businessbuddies

successful
assertive
management

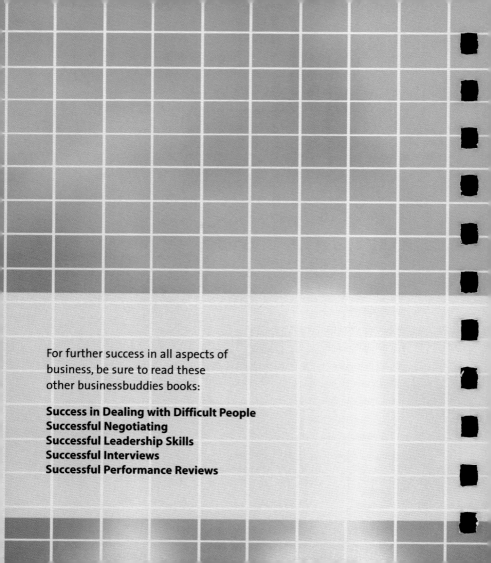

For further success in all aspects of
business, be sure to read these
other businessbuddies books:

Success in Dealing with Difficult People
Successful Negotiating
Successful Leadership Skills
Successful Interviews
Successful Performance Reviews

businessbuddies

successful
assertive
management

Ken Lawson, M.A., Ed.M.

BARRON'S

First edition for the United States, its territories and dependencies, and Canada
published 2006 by Barron's Educational Series, Inc.

Conceived and created by
Axis Publishing Limited
8c Accommodation Road
London NW11 8ED
www.axispublishing.co.uk

Creative Director: Siân Keogh
Editorial Director: Anne Yelland
Design: Sean Keogh, Simon de Lotz
Managing Editor: Conor Kilgallon
Production: Jo Ryan, Cécile Lerbière

NOTE: The opinions and advice expressed in this book are intended as a guide only. The publisher
and author accept no responsibility for any loss sustained as a result of using this book.

All inquiries should be addressed to:
Barron's Educational Series, Inc.
250 Wireless Boulevard
Hauppauge, New York 11788
www.barronseduc.com

Library of Congress Control No: 2005921777

ISBN-13: 978-0-7641-3247-6
ISBN-10: 0-7641-3247-4

Printed and bound in China
9 8 7 6 5 4 3 2 1

contents

Introduction

When it comes to getting your needs met in business circles, or almost any situation that involves a group of people, the shopworn adage that says that "the squeaky wheel gets the oil" very often rings true. But who are those squeaky wheels in our workplaces, and why do they feel it necessary to be the ones to make noise? Are they just attention-grabbing egotists who need to be the center of attention, or is there a point to their desire to be heard more often than not? And, is business success simply a matter of pushing oneself to be heard over the crowd, or do other factors come into play?

Success in interpersonal situations—whether in the workplace, in team settings, or in everyday life—begins with effectively expressing desired outcomes. The ability to express those outcomes, and the act of expressing them, is a large part of what we call assertive behavior, and it can be practiced by anyone, from senior executives to junior apprentices. Many leaders describe the process of driving toward a goal as executing a vision. And since executing that vision always involves other people, it is essential to articulate and execute it in a way that others can clearly hear, understand, and relate to.

Successful Assertive Management defines what it takes to reach your managerial goals and shows you exactly what you need to do and say to get your needs met effectively. You'll learn the crucial distinction between assertive and aggressive behaviors, and how they contrast with passive behaviors. You'll see how each of those behaviors affects you and those around you, whether bosses or subordinates. And you'll understand why assertive behavior is the cornerstone of your managerial success—in the short-term and over time.

You'll see that assertive behavior is not merely an increased level of verbalizing, or turning up the volume on your wishes and desires. Being assertive means cultivating a strong presence and conducting yourself with a confidence and aplomb that show the unmistakable signals of leadership.

Introduction continued

Through the ideas and insights in these pages, you'll understand that assertive behavior is the result of a distinctive point of view—a way of thinking that is oriented toward achievement.

Successful Assertive Management provides a wealth of practical strategies and guidelines for navigating key managerial situations. You'll find invaluable tips on developing assertive patterns of speaking: What to say when you need to get things done and how to say it. You'll learn how to carry yourself so that others can respond readily to your requests and direction—the body language that mirrors your leadership presence. And you'll find strategies for negotiating conflict; contributing to, and chairing, meetings; countering passive behavior; and making requests effectively.

You'll also read about the power of the positive inner voice and how to cultivate it to your benefit. You'll learn how to visualize achievement-oriented work images, and develop patterns of affirmative thinking. And you'll understand how and why success in the workplace is the natural outcome of thinking assertively—and how to transform your thoughts and visions into leadership actions.

Your success as a manager links directly to your ability to express your goals and needs. Your success in taking charge of that expression process in key workplace situations links directly to your ability to think and act assertively. With clear ideas and easy-to-understand strategies, this book shows you how to think, what to say, and what to do to have your way.

Ken Lawson, M.A., Ed.M.

Career management counselor and author

Instructor, School of Continuing and Professional Studies

New York University

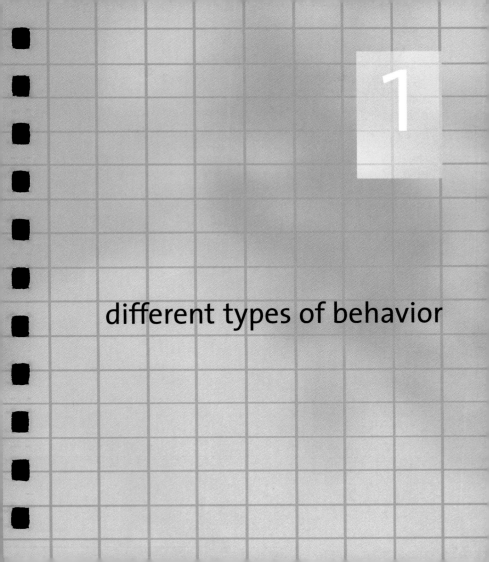

1

different types of behavior

different types of behavior

Benefits of assertiveness

Today's workplace is made up typically of much flatter hierarchical structures than in the past. Channels of communication between senior management and the rest of staff are more open and fluid. Employees are more ready to defend their legitimate rights. Leaders can no longer rely on their status, power, and rank to motivate subordinates. They must have excellent communication skills to transmit their desires and objectives in a way that's going to incite cooperation and willingness from their employees. In other words, they need to adopt assertive behavior. These are some of the many advantages that assertiveness brings to managers and their organizations:

1

ACCOMPLISH WHAT YOU DO WITHOUT GUILT
By recognizing that your needs and feelings are valid and letting other people know about them, you will be able to accomplish what you want to do without feeling you've been treading on other people's toes unfairly. Saying "no" is one of the most difficult things that managers face, and many will go to extreme lengths to avoid sounding negative or rejecting tasks and problems for fear of hurting others.

Assertiveness will improve your relationships with managers, subordinates, and colleagues so that you can act effectively without feeling guilty.

2 LEARN TO ACCEPT CRITICISM

Few managers or employees like to receive criticism. More often than not, people receiving criticism will respond defensively and then feel guilty about having felt angry. Assertive people can take criticism without taking it personally. They learn to distinguish between themselves and their actions or behaviors that may be under scrutiny. They try to learn from mistakes.

The most effective managers and employees can take criticism, accepting it when it is due.

different types of behavior
Benefits of assertiveness continued

3 MAKE UNPOPULAR DECISIONS
Many managers want to be liked and are unable to give constructive criticism, make a decision that will be opposed by the majority, or take more difficult steps like firing colleagues.

Assertiveness helps managers take necessary action without feeling that they will be personally judged. They can separate their organizations' objectives from their personal lives and convey to others that they are capable of doing so. This is likely to earn the respect of colleagues, who accept that decisions are being made without regard for personal feelings.

4 TAKE RISKS

Many companies' successes arise from managers who have made decisions with a considerable risk of failure. Assertive managers will stick their neck out for a plan that they think has a chance of reaping great benefits. These decisions will not be foolhardy or uncalculated actions but based on careful thought and made with a proper understanding of the dangers involved and the alternatives open in case of failure.

In many organizations, it is this ability to take risks that helps managers climb the ladder. Taking the safe option is not usually what senior managers are employed to do.

Overview of behavior types

There are two types of behavior that come naturally to most people because they are spontaneous responses learned from birth (see pp. 28–59):

1 AGGRESSIVE BEHAVIOR
Faced with a threat, people can chose to protect themselves by lashing out, perhaps violently, at the source of the fear.

2 PASSIVE BEHAVIOR
Or, when people are scared, there is also an animal instinct to retreat or hide.

THERE IS ALSO A THIRD TYPE, WHICH PEOPLE CAN LEARN:

3 ASSERTIVE BEHAVIOR
Unlike the other two responses, assertive behavior requires thought and a deliberate choice. Assertive people, experiencing the same threat as passive or aggressive people, look beyond the immediate situation and weigh up the consequences of retreat or retaliation, both to themselves and to others.

MAKING CHOICES

There are occasions when passive behavior is the most appropriate action, for instance in extreme cases when not retreating from a situation could implicate a great risk. Sometimes, during a takeover or a merger or a decision involving the stock market, there is no choice but to wait for another party to act.

On the other hand, aggression is sometimes necessary when swift, urgent action is the only way out. Most people tend to veer between both patterns of behavior as they are instinctive. A more considered choice is to behave assertively, which can be learned, practiced, developed, and perfected. To make the most informed choice and to be convinced of its greater effectiveness, it is important to understand more closely the three different types of behavior.

different types of behavior

What is assertive behavior?

1 Defining and defending one's owns rights and responsibilities at work.

2 Respecting the rights and responsibilities of others at work.

3 Being able to control feelings during a difficult or highly charged meeting.

4 Saying "no" to a request and giving the reasons for declining without feeling guilty.

5 Disagreeing with close colleagues without fearing that they will take the different opinions as a personal insult.

6 Backtracking on your original plan of action after listening to others who have pointed out reasonable objections.

7 Not being afraid of admitting to making mistakes.

8 Outlining problems and making them known to others without fear of repercussions.

9 Being able to listen without feeling pressured into coming up with an immediate solution.

10 Steering away from any behavior aimed at putting others down, such as open criticism in meetings, sarcasm, and shouting or swearing.

Why people choose assertive behavior

1

FAILURE OF ALTERNATIVE BEHAVIOR
They have always been passive or aggressive and realized that these two instinctive patterns of behavior, learned from childhood, are preventing them from achieving their objectives.

2

FREEDOM TO ACT
They have come to terms with their own responsibilities and know that it is in their hands to change their behavior. They are free to try to achieve what they like. The feeling of empowerment is empowering in itself and leads to greater motivation and achievement.

3 PEOPLE RESPOND BETTER

They have learned, often through trial and errors, that bullying people into being more productive or expecting staff to guess what they have to accomplish are two extreme ways of managing that don't yield results. Staff respond best to clear instructions that can be reasonably carried out.

4 SELF-RESPECT

They know who they are and what they want and are not ashamed of pursuing their dreams as long as they are not stepping on anyone else's toes or making unreasonable demands on others.

Effects of assertiveness on you

1 INCREASES SELF-CONFIDENCE
Handling a difficult situation successfully raises self-esteem and boosts the chances of behaving assertively in the future.

2 ENCOURAGES BETTER COMMUNICATION
When you are clear about what you want out of a situation, it will be much easier to transmit your needs to your staff. You'll be more confident about establishing open, honest dialog.

3 ENCOURAGES INITIATIVE
When you aren't afraid of making a mistake, you are more likely to try out new ideas even though these might not work. You are prepared to fail as long as you give it your best shot.

4 LESSENS GUILT

You will spend far less energy going through situations wondering if you overstepped the mark. You take responsibility for your actions and don't look back.

5 IMPROVES TEAM RELATIONS

By stating clearly what you want and by not resorting to either bullying or indecision, you make your team feel more comfortable with your plans and create a better working environment. Team members respect your decisions and respond positively to your requests. Knowing that you are acting even-handedly with everybody and singling out people for tasks on the basis of who is most suited, fosters collaboration and respect among team members.

Effects of assertiveness on you continued

6 ENSURES THAT PEOPLE WON'T TAKE ADVANTAGE
Passive people can sometimes be viewed as weak and people will use that to manipulate them. Assertive managers state clearly their intentions and won't tolerate being messed around.

7 REDUCES STRESS
The less time you spend thinking about how others are responding to your behavior, the less time you spend feeling tense or nervous. That management can be stressful is a given, but assertive managers will not be stressed by minor worries, as the consensus they build around themselves eliminates such stress.

8 IMPROVES PERSPECTIVE
Assertiveness makes you less prone to react to rude or
impolite comments or put downs. You won't be so sensitive
to others' opinions because you have a clearer perspective of
the big picture.

9 GENERATES GREATER CONTROL
Faced with aggressive behavior, you are going to respond
calmly and help take the heat out of a potentially
explosive situation.

10 CREATES MORE FREEDOM
You will rid yourself of any negative inner voices that incite
self-doubt and lack of confidence.

26
Effects of assertiveness on others

1 BETTER UNDERSTANDING
They know exactly where they stand with you because you have explained yourself clearly and with no hidden agendas.

2 MORE FEEDBACK
They will be encouraged by your self-confidence in raising objections or expressing their own needs and opinions. With less assertive managers, people tend to hide their ideas, which could be of great benefit to the company.

3 FASTER INFORMATION FLOW
They will volunteer more information about a project, however trivial that might seem.

4 MORE EFFECTIVE PROBLEM SOLVING
As colleagues or subordinates are more ready to share information, then you can make more informed decisions.

5   CONFIDENT STAFF
The overall atmosphere of a team led by an assertive manager
is of cooperation and self-confidence to carry out a project.
These qualities enhance the chances of success.

6   DEFINITION OF LIMITS
Co-workers who like to step the line or push managers to the
limit to test their resilience will be discouraged by an assertive
manager who defines proper boundaries and ground rules
that they can understand and appreciate.

7   ENCOURAGEMENT
A boss who knows what he wants can encourage previously
unmotivated staff to work to higher standards because
they know that extra hard work will be appreciated, if not
rewarded. In fact, many people are not in jobs for the rewards
but for the notice and appreciation that comes from a job
well done.

What is aggressive behavior?

Aggressive behavior is most often mistaken for assertive behavior and vice versa, mainly because both are more obviously active forms of responses than passive behavior. The characteristics of aggression however are considerably different from assertiveness and can be listed as:

1

ASSERTIVE BEHAVIOR
Unlike passive or aggressive responses, assertive behavior requires thought and a deliberate choice. Assertive people who are experiencing the same threat as passive or aggressive people look beyond the immediate situation and weigh up the consequences of retreat or retaliation, both to themselves and to others.

2

WIN-LOSE MENTALITY
An aggressive person seeks to win an argument or a point at the expense of the other person (i.e., the other person has to lose, whatever the situation or argument.) There is no attempt at genuine problem solving, simply point scoring.

3 PUTTING OWN NEEDS FIRST
Aggressive behavior means putting one's own needs and
opinions first and making sure these are known to others,
without respect or understanding as to how these wants will
impact others.

4 DISMISSING OTHERS' RIGHTS
The rights of other people are usually not considered and are
sometimes violated by aggressive behavior.

5 FINDING FAULT
Aggressive people are quick to pounce on other people's
mistakes, especially if they think it makes them superior.

What is aggressive behavior? continued

THERE ARE TWO BASIC TYPES OF AGGRESSIVE BEHAVIOR:

1 DIRECT AGGRESSION IS MANIFESTED BY:

ANGER: Difficult situations tend to provoke explosive anger in aggressive people. The anger can be threatening and have no control or direction.

SHOUTING: A symptom of anger aimed at overwhelming the other person, is shouting.

HOSTILE BODY LANGUAGE: Fist pumping and finger pointing are examples of aggressive people using nonverbal behavior to intimidate the opponent.

SWEARING: The use of foul or inappropriate language marks a complete lack of control.

INTERRUPTIONS: Aggressive people will make it clear they don't value what you have to say and so have no qualms about interrupting.

2 INDIRECT AGGRESSION IS SHOWN BY:

SARCASM: People who want to make a point without being straightforward use sarcasm.

MOODINESS: Sulkiness or sudden silences are used to create an uneasy atmosphere.

EMOTIONAL BLACKMAIL: Colleagues can threaten to become ill or burst into tears when confronted with a difficult task or criticism.

UNEXPLAINED BEHAVIOR: Deep sighing, refusing to look their co-worker in the eye, and slamming doors all aim at displaying dissatisfaction without using clear statements.

Why are people aggressive?

There are several reasons behind the use of frequent aggressive behavior:

1 SPECIFIC SCENARIOS

Aggression is highly prized and actively encouraged in certain high-profile jobs. This is particularly true in the case of managers who are hired to carry out a significant number of redundancies or even to close down an entire division. They could also be introducing a new operating system or management style that has already been approved at a senior level and that merely needs to be implemented, regardless of the opinions of the majority of the staff. These jobs are often of a temporary nature, with the manager who has overseen the firing of staff moving on to a new assignment once the most painful changes have occurred. Diplomacy and bridge-building skills are not seen as essential in these cases. Even if the aggressive practices start affecting the workplace, the manager in question may have moved on so reprisals or a backlash are more difficult. The problem occurs when such aggressive styles are transferred to other parts of the business where a more consensual approach is required.

2 DEFENSE MECHANISM
When managers feel under particular threat, they may anticipate any perceived or real trouble by attacking the source instead of carefully thinking about what measure would be most appropriate.

3 STRIKE FIRST
An aggressive person may strike first as a means of avoiding potential conflict: "Shout before you are shouted at." This is unproductive in the short and long term. It is more helpful to reach a consensus on what the problem is, how it can be resolved, and who is the most effective person to resolve it than to put off facing it through self interest.

Why are people aggressive? continued

4 COMPENSATION FOR PASSIVE BEHAVIOR
It's not unusual for passive people who have taken on more
work than they can handle by being too fearful of making a
fuss or who have been on the receiving end of aggressive
behavior to have a sudden outburst of anger. This surprising
display of aggressive behavior is often not directed at the
original source of aggression but at other passive workers.

5 FEELINGS OF INFERIORITY
People who are unhappy with themselves or feel inadequate
about their work think aggression will raise their self-esteem
or at least get them noticed. It may do this in the short term
but the long-term effects on themselves and on those around
them will be negative.

6 PERSONAL WORRIES

Aggressive outbursts can be linked with personal or family worries that incite quick temper and lack of focused thinking. The fact is that outside concerns should have no place in the workplace, but all too often they do: An argument with a partner or child gets replayed in the work situation for example, or a financial worry leads to a retort of the "you think you have problems" variety. This is unhealthy for everybody concerned.

different types of behavior
Effects of aggressive behavior

When you are aggressive, whether it is your normal behavior or not, there are inevitable consequences:

1

SHORT-TERM RELIEF
You can feel relieved by getting something out of your system, even a sense of well-being at having released pent-up anger. If an outburst of anger has achieved a desired result, you may be tempted to use aggression in the future. It is important to weigh the advantages and disadvantages of an instance of aggressive behavior and to assess whether the relief is merely short-lived and temporary.

2

GUILT
In the cases where you've had an outburst only to vent your feelings and without any concrete results, you are likely to be overcome with feelings of guilt and remorse at things that you said in the heat of the moment and that you will most probably regret.

3 STRESS

People often complain of increased heart rate, deeper breathing, and sometimes shaking and trembling, after a display of hostility. This only contributes to the likely stress that caused the outburst in the first place. With a tense body following a loud argument, it will certainly be more difficult to concentrate.

4 SELF-DOUBT

People who are not naturally aggressive or who show aggression infrequently can begin to doubt their own responses to problems. Knowing that aggression is not the answer, they question their responses to situations that are really clear-cut.

Effects of aggressive behavior continued

5 LOSS OF SELF-RESPECT
Feelings of shame and self-degradation that follow aggressive behavior are further negative consequences.

6 WEAKNESS
Your position in the company can be considerably weakened if your act of aggression was over a mistake or a misunderstanding that could easily have been settled another way. For example, you publicly blame a subordinate for something that arose from an error of judgment on your part rather than accepting the truth of the situation. When the truth comes out, as it will, your action will weaken your position in the eyes of your employees, and probably others, and any future decisions you try to implement will become more difficult.

7 ISOLATION

Nobody responds easily to aggression. They are likely to match your hostility with their own direct anger or pent up hostility that may work against your meeting objectives. You may feel put upon or under fire by staff and find yourself bereft of allies.

8 PASSIVE BEHAVIOR

When aggression has failed, paradoxically people may withdraw into their shells and adopt passive behavior that brings a new set of problems.

The effects on others

1 ANGER
Aggressive behavior inevitably encourages a response laced with an equal dose of anger. Once employees' backs are put up, they are far less likely to cooperate with your objectives.

2 RESENTMENT
Feelings of revenge are common among staff who have been at the ugly end of an attack, particularly if they've been scolded or reprimanded in public. They will be far more intent on exacting revenge than on doing the job in hand.

3 RESISTANCE
Once frustrated employees take steps to express their resentment, managers may face active resistance to their leadership.

4 FEAR

The more passive employees faced with an aggressive manager that they don't dare stand up to are going to put more energy into protecting themselves from the next attack than on their work. If they are experiencing any problems that they should be pointing out to the manager, they may be reluctant to report them for fear of reprisal.

5 LACK OF COMMUNICATION

Passive people may also start withholding vital information from managers as a way of making life difficult for the managers. Managers will no longer be able to trust them and may spend valuable time that should be devoted to their own job eliciting information that a more reasonable person could expect to be receiving as a matter of course. This cycle of distrust can be highly divisive.

The effects on others continued

6 NO INITIATIVE
Fear or resentment will discourage staff from coming up with new ideas.

7 POOR TEAM SPIRIT
A combination of scared, resentful, and threatened staff is not conducive to a cooperative team spirit.

8 JOB CHANGES
Talented and hard-working staff may be tempted to change department or company if they are no longer prepared to put up with consistent aggressive behavior.

9 IN-FIGHTING

Managers who behave aggressively to each other encourage unhealthy competition that is more about scoring points against each other than achieving better results for the company as a whole.

10 CONFUSION

Employees at the receiving end of indirect aggression like sarcasm or sulking will feel confused as to the exact nature of the problem. Confusion can easily turn to hurt and feeling of being manipulated, both of which are unhealthy and have no place in the working environment.

What is passive behavior?

Passive behavior can also be known as nonassertive behavior and tends to include the following characteristics:

1

FAILURE TO DEFEND RIGHTS
Passive behavior means that people fail to stand up for their own rights. They may not even know that they have rights to defend. This encourages selfish people to take advantage of them.

2

SELF-EFFACEMENT
Even when passive people are aware of their rights and ability to make an effective contribution to a discussion, and they manage to express any opinions or beliefs, they do so in a diffident, cautious way that encourages others to ignore or disregard them. This reinforces their unwillingness to contribute to discussions, since their contributions are so frequently disregarded.

3 LACK OF DIRECTNESS

Passive people won't be open about their feelings and wants. They won't complain about poor products or service, either deflecting an enquiry ("I had some trouble setting it up," in response to a question on how something is working) or not telling the truth ("The meal was great, thank you," when most of the meal is returned to the kitchen uneaten).

4 NO RESPONSIBILITY

Passive people seem to share little sense of responsibility for their actions because they appear at the mercy of other people's decisions or others' demands for their rights. This can make them appear to be victims who are unable or unwilling to see that their own actions may in fact have contributed or caused the problem.

5 SELF-PITY

An extension of a victim persecution can extend to self-pity that nothing can change for them. This means that when passive people miss a deadline or make a mistake at work, they can attribute it to their regular bad luck or inability to change their lot.

6 LOW ENERGY

Feelings of powerlessness will be accompanied by low energy levels. Passive people have little motivation for active, purposeful work if they don't think they can make much difference. Low energy levels can be "catching," with previously motivated individuals underperforming under the influence of the passive individual.

7 PEOPLE PLEASER

Passive people's tendency to put other people's wishes first makes them superficially attractive to managers because they are easily convinced of a certain decision or plan of action. They won't raise any objections for fear of angering the decision maker. They will avoid conflict at any cost and promise to do things even if they won't be able to follow through.

The people pleaser who agrees to implement a new system in his department to his superior, who knows he will face opposition from his own staff, for example, is helping no one, including himself.

Why choose passive behavior?

People adopt passive behavior regularly for the following reasons:

1

THE WILL TO PLEASE

Many passive people think that by pleasing other people and putting their needs first, they will be rewarded by having their needs eventually seen to. This pattern of behavior is very common among young children who are constantly told that if they do what their parents do, they will be rewarded with special attention. When this ingrained pattern is transferred to the workplace, the employer has few incentives to follow through her end of the bargain with the employee who is eager to please. Yet there are many occasions, when staff members believe that if they only work hard enough, they will be appreciated and get their just reward. This only sets up frustration. An employee who starts to feel undervalued as his hard work goes unnoticed and unrewarded may choose to move on, only to repeat the cycle elsewhere.

2 FEAR OF REJECTION
Another consequence of behavior patterns learned during
infancy is that bad behavior will be punished by rejection
or less attention. People who desist from expressing their
opinions or raising objections to new plans or projects are
in fear of being rejected or of being branded a difficult
team player.

3 LACK OF CONFIDENCE
Low self-esteem can lead people to avoid the spotlight at work.
The upshot is that passive people will say little in meetings,
provide no feedback on projects that they are involved in, and
end up being overlooked for challenging new tasks.

4 NEGATIVE THOUGHTS

Passive people can feel paralyzed about taking any action by self-defeating mind games like "I've never been good with numbers" or "me and computers have never gotten along." They may also have labeled themselves as useless at specific tasks from an early stage and can't see that it lies within their power to improve themselves.

5 INABILITY TO ACT

Following on from negative thoughts is the inability to act. In the belief that they are "no good with figures," they do nothing to improve their understanding. Similarly, a person who believes himself computer illiterate will not undertake the simplest "where to start" instructions and be powerless to even switch it on.

6

EXCESSIVE EMPATHY
Although it is appropriate to take other people's feelings into consideration, empathy can lead people to assume too much responsibility for other people's feelings if they get hurt.

7

POLITENESS
Some people tend to confuse speaking their mind about a subject as rudeness. They think being regarded as considerate will be more valued than raising a valid objection. Managers and fellow workers, however, deserve the respect of a considered opinion, even if it is contrary to prevailing views.

The effects on you

1 SHORT-TERM RELIEF
By avoiding a potentially difficult situation with a boss or work colleagues, passive people will feel released from trouble and pain. They feel they are off the hook.

2 PRIDE
By taking on an assignment or task that a boss was finding difficult to assign, the eager-to-please employee can feel proud about being helpful. However, this may well set up the expectation of reward, which is unlikely to be forthcoming and will lead to problems further down the line as resentment sets in.

3 SELF-PITY

Passive people who have agreed to take on extra work without fuss can then realize they have taken on more than they can chew and feel sorry for themselves. They don't realize that it was in their power to say "no." They think they are always picked on and pressured into accepting extra tasks.

4 ENVY

They can also feel jealous that other colleagues never seem to be singled out by the boss. They think this is a matter of luck, not of choice. Deliberately or not, a boss who knows she has a yes man on her team is going to single him out, rather than either motivate another employee to help or to apportion the workload more evenly.

The effects on you continued

5 POWERLESSNESS
The inability to change the course of events at work can create passive people who are trapped into a pattern that they cannot get out of.

6 ANGER
Mounting frustration will eventually lead to sudden bouts of anger that will in turn make the passive person, unused to being aggressive, feel guilty about losing control.

7 BOREDOM
Unable to change their work situation, passive people will start failing to engage with their work and even start making mistakes that will only make them an easy prey to more aggressive managers or co-workers.

8 DEPRESSION

Once the feeling of powerlessness becomes natural, passive people can develop problems like backaches and headaches, and start to take frequent days off sick. These problems may be real, but equally likely they are symptoms of underlying depression, which contributes further to feelings of powerlessness and self-pity.

9 TENSION

In spite of the temporary relief experienced after not confronting a difficult boss or colleague, tension mounts up because the original source of the difficulty has not been tackled. People worrying about unresolved issues can't focus on their work properly. They need to resolve the situation and move on rather than dwell on it. Instead, they may start to exhibit symptoms of stress and depression, which can also manifest themselves in sick days.

The effects on others

1 LACK OF ENERGY
Working with passive people can become tiring. Their lack of
energy and enthusiasm can end up being contagious
especially if all efforts to enthuse and motivate them are met
with continuous blank expressions or noncommittal answers.

2 DEMOTIVATION
A passive boss who fails to make clear decisions or to establish
clearly her objectives and those of her team with her own
superiors leaves a team without direction. Staff morale can
begin to disintegrate as people despair about a job ever
getting finished properly. This in turn contributes to the
situation in which a job is not finished properly because the
mindset says it will not be. Clear direction motivates people
to succeed.

3 FEELING OF SUPERIORITY
Less sensitive colleagues can easily start feeling superior and
smug that they are better at handling difficult situations than
passive people. This can encourage the more aggressive
people to take advantage of the passive people in the future.

4 PITY
Passive people who are unable to stand up for themselves or
to say "no" can inspire pity in colleagues who do stand up for
their rights.

5 GUILT
Pity can soon develop into guilt if a person remains passive for
an extended period of time.

6 ANGER

Nobody likes to feel guilty, and feeling guilty borders on being passive because it assumes too much responsibility for somebody else's actions. In the end, you can end up feeling frustrated and angry with colleagues who fail to stand up for their rights.

7 LACK OF RESPECT

It becomes difficult to respect people who won't assert themselves. Knowing that a manager is going to react to situations passively, his team members also understand that he is not going to support them and their needs. This contributes still further to the lack of respect.

8 FEWER INITIATIVES
In a company scenario, the failure by senior managers to make
decisions encourages passivity among the workforce and
stops staff from coming up with new ideas or initiatives.

9 BUILD-UP OF PROBLEMS
Passive management is storing up trouble as difficult
situations are avoided.

10 LOSS OF STAFF
Once problems mount up, workers who are seeking to work in
a dynamic, well-organized company with clear objectives, are
likely to switch jobs.

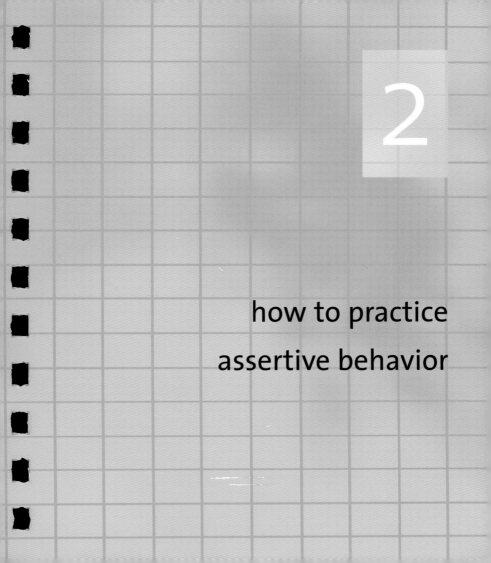

2

how to practice assertive behavior

Different verbal behavior

Identifying the various verbal characteristics of the three main behavioral types should help you adopt talking techniques that make you more assertive.

FEATURES OF ASSERTIVE TALK

The verbal behavior of assertive people reflects confidence and clarity. These people stand up for their rights but are also sensitive to other people's rights. These are some characteristics:

1

"I" STATEMENTS

Using "I" statements can be confused with aggression and a strong ego but only when they are accompanied with unreasonable or dismissive opinions and relayed in a loud tone of voice. Otherwise, an "I" statement shows that the speaker takes full responsibility for her opinion. For instance, "I think it is a good idea" defines the speaker's opinion more clearly and decisively than "Don't you think it's a good idea?" Other instances of "I" statements such as "I feel angry when..." or "I want" show conviction and directness. There is no intention of hiding behind bland statements such as "The company believes it is better...."

2 BRIEF, CORE PHRASES

Speaking in clear, direct, unambiguous sentences helps the assertive person to put his point across effectively. The next time you want to appear assertive, think of a core phrase that expresses your message in as few words as possible. Get rid of any padding. If you have various messages to communicate, form several core phrases, but keep them separate. The best way to learn to do this effectively is to listen to other people who you consider good communicators. Some politicians rely on spin, but the more effective are those who get two or three key points across to people who hear what is said and immediately understand and "get" the message.

Different verbal behavior continued

3 JARGON

People who keep changing their words and phrases according to the people they are talking to are sometimes accused of being inconsistent. However an assertive person who wants to make her message clear should be aware of her speaker and change her vocabulary if the other person may be unfamiliar with certain technical or management jargon. Creating a gap between the speaker and the receiver is hardly effective communication.

4 ASSUMPTIONS

Never assume that other people automatically have the same points of reference as you. You can't expect other people to read your mind. It's better to spell things out than to withhold information.

5 QUESTIONS

Showing that they respect the rights of others, assertive people not only make direct, honest statements, but also ask questions to find out what others think. They ask open questions that will encourage others to express their opinions.

6 ANSWERS

Assertive people are also not afraid to answer questions, even if they know their listeners are not going to like what they hear. The old adage of honesty being the best policy, however, works. If you have to deliver an unpopular message in reply to a question, do so simply and honestly, then invite more questions. This assertive approach will win respect.

7 GENERALIZATIONS
Assertive people don't assume that everyone thinks alike so they won't make sweeping statements like "most people would agree that" or "everyone knows that this won't work." They are careful about distinguishing opinions and facts.

8 CRITICISM OF BEHAVIOR, NOT PERSON
Eager to stick to the facts and to things that can be changed, an assertive person will focus on a particular aspect of another person's behavior that is bothering him. He won't attack the person. For instance, if a co-worker is constantly late, he may say: "I see you're having trouble coming in on time," which gives room for change, as opposed to: "You're late again!" which puts the other person on the defensive.

9 SUGGESTIONS

The assertive person may have made up her mind on an issue but instead of heavy-handed advice like "It's clearly better to," she may opt for "Do you think it would be better if...." That allows the other person to make up his own mind.

10 CONSENSUS

The assertive person does not see listening to others but making up his own mind as being weak. By listening to his team, for example, a leader shows respect. The team is more likely to accept a decision, even if they don't like it, if they feel their views have been canvassed. They may even buy into it being a majority decision.

Different verbal behavior continued

FEATURES OF AGGRESSIVE TALK
Aggressive people's verbal behavior will reflect a strong belief in their own rights and needs but not in those of others. These are some characteristics of aggressive talk.

1 FORCEFUL INSTRUCTIONS
The person will try to control others through the use of commands like "It has to be done immediately" or "Fetch me the documents."

2 OPINIONS DISGUISED AS FACTS
The person's judgment will be expressed as a fact: "Everyone knows that that way of doing things doesn't work" or "Ask anyone, and they'll tell you the same."

3 HEAVY USE OF "I" STATEMENT

Although "I" statements, used at appropriate moments are assertive, when they are used liberally they indicate a self-centered speaker. Phrases like "I know it will work" and "In my experience, it's always worked like that" are aimed at discouraging any challenge. This is not helpful, makes employees reluctant to contribute and can foster feelings of resentment, rather than feelings of collaboration, trust, and respect.

4

GENERAL BLAME
Angry statements about how things have gone generally
wrong because of other people's behavior are typical of
aggressive people. The critical statements rarely tend to focus
on a specific subject, which makes it even more difficult to
argue against.

5

SARCASM
When they don't criticize you directly, aggressive people can
resort to sniping or sarcasm to put you down. This can be
intensely wearing, partly because you have no way of knowing
when it's going to strike next.

6 RHETORICAL COMMENTS
These tend to be based on assumptions that the other person
has done something wrong. For instance, "I suppose you've
forgotten to bring those figures" or "You obviously didn't finish
the assignment did you?"

7 STRONG ADVICE
Aggressive people never miss an opportunity to give advice
that tends to be in the form of "I know better." The advice
comes across more as a reason for promoting their skills than
as a genuine attempt at helping the other person. There are
lots of "should" and "ought" words sprinkled in the advice.

FEATURES OF PASSIVE TALK

Nonassertive people tend to use verbal behavior that shows they are unaware of their rights and needs and if they do, they don't know how to stand up for them. The following are characteristics:

1 PROFUSE APOLOGIES

Awkward and frequent apologies are common among certain types of passive people. People who use "I'm sorry to disturb you" phrases are either excessively polite or very uncertain of themselves.

2 SELF PUT-DOWNS

Some passive people like to tell people how useless they are at a certain activity or chores or how they never seem to get anything right. People usually respond by trying to shore them up, giving them a pitying pat on the back or exhibiting sheer annoyance at the person for not trying to improve her skills.

3 SELF-PITY
"If only" is a phrase that passive people use quite frequently to lament a moment in the past when they failed to act assertively. Regretting the past is not constructive.

4 SELF-IMPOSED CONSTRAINTS
These consist of a certain number of activities that the person must accomplish within a certain time and punishes himself if he hasn't achieved them. Typical self-talk phrases are "I ought to" or "I should" that have guilt-ridden connotations. They also make the speaker appear compelled to carry out tasks at the will of other forces. It is far more forceful for instance to say "I will complete by x."

Different verbal behavior continued

5

RAMBLING SPEECH PATTERNS
Long, rambling sentences that go on incoherently and without direction display nerves and a lack of confidence.

6

SILENCE
Saying nothing is another choice for passive people. This can come across as aggressive because it leaves others in the dark about the person's real needs and opinions. This is a classic behavior of people who cannot communicate their wants and needs effectively: rather than be imprecise or tie themselves up in knots, they take the option of saying nothing.

7 HESITATION

The speaker tends to start a sentence, stop, and then start again. His speech is peppered with "Ers" and "Uhs." There are many pauses as if the speaker is waiting for the listener to fill in the gaps.

8 NEGATIVITY

The word "can't" best reveals the self-doubt of passive people. Next time you're tempted to use the word "can't" try to find a substitute that sounds more positive. If you have to decline an invitation for a drink because you have too much work to do, don't say "I can't." You will sound far less powerless if you say "I'd love to, but I have some work to do so I won't."

how to practice assertive behavior

Assertive delivery

Verbal behavior is not limited to the careful choice of words and phrases. A confident delivery can make a major difference to the impact of statements. The following are features worth considering during exchanges:

1 VOLUME
Aggressive people think that shouting louder will enhance their messages, although the effect is that the listener is distracted by the unnecessarily high decibels or is put off by the loudness that suggests a ticking off.

2 PASSIVE BEHAVIOR
Some people tend to speak in hushed tones to minimize what, in their eyes, appears to be an aggressive statement. Listeners either are confused by the contradiction between the severity of the statement and the light delivery or simply can't hear the statement. This can be unhelpful: it is more effective to speak clearly and confidently. An audience has the right to hear what is being said, even if the speaker knows that what he is saying will be unpopular.

3 ASSERTIVE BEHAVIOR
Assertive speakers take into account the context and the
listener before deciding on the volume of their delivery. This
shows they are sensitive about the people around them and
respectful of their rights. For instance, during a meeting with
frequent interruptions and heated discussions, it will be
appropriate to raise the volume without shouting. On the
other hand, confronted with an angry co-worker, responding in
a low-pitched, relaxed way will show that the speaker is in
control and not responding emotionally to the outburst.

4 SPEED
If you are feeling nervous, the chances are you might speed up
delivery, and your listeners will find it difficult to keep up with
you or switch off because the fast speed can suggest you are
in a hurry and your message is not that important.

Assertive delivery continued

5 PITCH
When people are tense, their voices tend to rise in pitch. Squeaky voices don't sound authoritative. Try to keep your pitch low.

6 PROJECTION
Projection of the voice, especially during a meeting or presentation, doesn't require loudness alone but plenty of intonation. It is important that the appropriate emphasis be put on key words. Reading through a presentation several times beforehand, preferably in front of a colleague, is useful to make sure the right light and shade is used and that pauses are used effectively.

7 TIMBRE
When people are under stress, voices are thin and seem to come from the throat. Try to bring your voice from the diaphragm or the belly. The voice will automatically sound fuller and more resonant.

SIX POINTS TO CHECK BEFORE DELIVERING A LONG SPEECH

1 Have you cleared your throat?

2 Do you have a glass of water close by?

3 Take short, quick breaths before the speech and longer ones during delivery.

4 Maintain regular eye contact with the audience.

5 Don't speed read through the speech. You may know it by heart, but the listeners are listening to it for the first time.

6 Pause for emphasis after key points.

how to practice assertive behavior

Different ways of listening

Assertive statements delivered confidently won't have any impact without the attention of a listener. It's likely that an assertive talker also has good listening skills. Listening makes up half the communication process and is key to effective planning and problem solving, so why are so many people poor listeners?

1

AGGRESSIVE
Aggressive listeners are too busy thinking of their own rights and are more concerned with what they are going to say next than to acknowledge that other people have the right to communicate. As they tend to have fixed opinions, they are also selective listeners, noticing words that will support their interpretation of what is being said rather than actually listening to the words. The signs that they are not listening are a lack of eye contact, few visual signs of listening such as gentle nodding of the head, signs of boredom such as yawning and frequent interruptions. The sound of their own voice in rebuttal is more important than the consideration they should be offering other people.

2 PASSIVE

Passive listeners are expected to be effective listeners because they tend to put other people's rights before their own. In fact, they are so overly concerned with what others are thinking about them or how they are expected to respond that the focus is on their own behavior rather than on really listening to what others are saying.

3 ASSERTIVE

Assertive listeners make sure they are attentive and alert while others speak. Even if they have certain views on the subject, they will try not to express these until others have made clear their views and needs. They will try not to interrupt unless it is to ask a question to sort out a confusion (which shows they are actively listening) or to prompt the other person to expand on a point.

Becoming an effective listener

1 MAKE EYE CONTACT
Have you ever tried to tell someone something important and their eyes are wandering around the room or busy skim reading a report? To avoid this off-putting habit, make sure you maintain regular eye contact with the speaker, but don't fix your gaze constantly as this becomes intimidating.

2 STAY STILL
Fidgeting with papers, a bag, or a cellphone are signs of distraction. Remain relaxed and alert. If you are distracted, you won't hear what is being said and could miss key points. For example, you will hear the conclusion that has been reached but not the reasons why such a course of action has been decided on. This can set up feelings of resentment, which are misplaced. As you have a right to be heard, you have a duty to listen, too.

3 ENCOURAGE

Make intermittent gestures to show you are following the speaker. Gestures include smiles, "yes" and "no," raising eyebrows to show surprise, and nods. Don't exaggerate the gestures as they will suggest you are actually bored.

4 MAKE MENTAL NOTES

Try to draw out a few main points from the other's exchange as this will help you sort out what is important about the other's message. Distinguish between facts and opinions. If the speaker is rambling or nervous and the messages are unclear, you can ask yourself a few questions to get a clearer picture:

■ Why is she telling me this now?
■ How is she feeling about telling me?
■ Does she want me to act in a particular way?

Becoming an effective listener continued

5 PARAPHRASE

When the speaker has finished, you can show you have been actively listening while repeating back in your own words and rather more briefly, their main points. This is also a way of checking you have understood the other person. Phrases such as "Am I correct that you are suggesting..." "You think our next course of action should be..." and "I think your suggestion that we try to do this..." all show that you have been listening, have heard what has been said, and understand the message. A speaker in this situation can be confident that his listeners understand his intention.

Alternatively, if your paraphrase is not what the speaker intended, the misunderstanding can be corrected immediately and work can proceed smoothly.

6 KNOW WHEN TO INTERRUPT
In principle, it is better to keep interruptions to a minimum
as they stop the natural flow of the speaker. Frequent
interruptions also tend to give the impression that you don't
want to listen and are too focused on your own needs.
Sometimes, though, it is necessary to interject. For instance, if
the speaker is veering off the subject, you may intervene with
a few key words of the main message to get the speaker back
on track. Or if you strongly disagree with a statement or
opinion that is not part of the main message, you may want
to make your viewpoint clear. Finally, you may want to verify
that you have understood a specific part of the argument that
needs clearing up immediately.

7 SHOW EMPATHY

Try to cast your own views aside for a while and concentrate on seeing the situation from the other person's point of view. Showing empathy is sometimes referred to as "nondirective listening" because you are literally not directing or channeling the other person's thought in a direction. You are giving the person the respect to find her own direction. She may have no specific objective other than to unload her feelings. If this is the case, listening with attention but without reaction may help her to reach a decision or formulate an opinion. At the very least, it says that someone is prepared to hear her out.

8 LIMIT OPINIONS

Unless you have been asked specifically for an opinion, don't feel compelled to come up with a solution or immediate response. Imparting advice and a personal take on a statement can come across as bossy and intrusive. In most business situations, there are forums for discussion when opinions are actively sought. This is the time to offer personal opinions. If you are not asked for them, they really play no part in making you an effective listener. Always consider your position from the other side of the coin: if you are speaking, do you expect your audience to offer their opinions? If you do not, then you should not offer them either. When your opinion is actively sought, that is the time to offer it. This shows respect for the speaker.

Becoming an effective listener continued

9 AVOID HOOKS

Listening and responding sympathetically to other viewpoints are parts of assertive listening, but there are some potential dangers. The speaker may try to weaken your own point of view and try to pull you into his logic. He may also try to sidetrack you from the main business you are trying to focus on. These gambits are also called hooks. The most effective way of not getting hooked is to paraphrase back what the person is telling you to show that you are listening and then to use a core phrase that outlines your position. That tells the speaker you are not prepared to be drawn into an argument or to labor over an irrelevant point at this stage.

10 MATCH

Empathic listening can sometimes lead to making subtle adjustments to your own behavior to blend in as much as possible with the other speaker. This does not mean relinquishing your own views or personality. If done skillfully, it can be a way of creating a closer rapport with the listener. Matching or blending involves quickly identifying the language of the other person, the speed of the delivery, and the loudness of the voice. For instance, if you are dealing with a soft-spoken person who likes to think before speaking and has a slow delivery, you may have to tone down your naturally loud, fast way of talking. People are far more likely to respect your views when you mirror and match theirs.

how to practice assertive behavior

Types of body language

RECOGNIZING DIFFERENT TYPES OF BODY LANGUAGE

The most assertive verbal skills can lose their impact if the speaker's body language fails to reinforce the main message. Body language must be compatible with words and delivery for successful assertive behavior. Very often, a listener's immediate impressions of a speaker are governed by the way he is saying things rather than what he is actually saying.

An examination of the different types of body language is helpful to either adopt body language that is going to help drive a point home or to avoid certain mannerisms that will lessen the impact of a potentially vital statement.

FEATURES OF ASSERTIVE BODY LANGUAGE

1   GESTURES
    ■ Open hand movements encourage others to speak.

    ■ A head that is held up high (but not too high) shows determination.

    ■ Showing the palms of the hands indicates the speaker has nothing to hide.

    ■ Leaning forward toward the other person (but at a distance that respects the other's personal space) usually invites a closer rapport.

Types of body language continued

2 FACIAL EXPRESSION
- Eye contact is direct and regular but never fixed, which can be intimidating.

- Smiles are used with discretion and include the eyes.

- Jaw is relaxed.

- Frowns are used sparingly and only to effect appropriate displeasure or disapproval.

3 POSTURE
- Upright, calm open stance suggests readiness to confront the world and leap into action.

- Hands hanging loosely at the side and kept from crossing or jerking around help to create the impression of a relaxed person who is at ease.

THE SIGNS OF AGGRESSIVE BEHAVIOR INCLUDE:

1 GESTURES

- Finger pointing harks back to the action of teachers or parents telling small children off.

- Fist thumping, which is associated with sportsmen whose main goal is to win at the expense of the other person, is an admirable quality in sports but not appropriate within an office team environment.

- Standing upright with the head in the air can denote distance and arrogance.

- Walking around in long strides shows impatience.

- Crossed arms looks defensive literally.

- Invading personal space, by standing too close to another person, can be intimidating.

- Turning abruptly away from the other person is dismissive.

- A waving hand while the other person is talking is disrespectful.

- An unexpected touch or pat at an inappropriate moment can be patronizing.

Types of body language continued

2 FACIAL EXPRESSIONS

■ An upturned smile that doesn't reach the eyes, comes across as sneering.

■ An exaggerated roll of the eyes can appear sarcastic or dismissive.

■ Glazed eyes suggest boredom.

■ A tightly set jaw looks threatening.

■ Frowning reveals disapproval.

■ Eyebrows raised in amazement can be undermining.

■ Chin thrust forward shows inflexibility.

■ Squinting eyes reveal contempt.

■ A taut look about the mouth suggests tension.

3 POSTURE

■ A rigid, erect back with hands on hips can be defensive.

■ Tight fists show anger.

■ Elbows that point out look poised for assault.

■ Hunched shoulders are defensive.

■ Tight shoulders spell tension.

■ Folded arms can be defensive or even hostile.

■ Not meeting a person head on but standing sideways or even half turned away is dismissive.

Types of body language continued

THE SIGNS OF PASSIVE BEHAVIOR ARE:

1 GESTURES

■ A hand covering the mouth shows lack of self-confidence.

■ Constant fiddling with hair or clothes is self-conscious behavior.

■ Elbows and knees pulled toward the body.

■ Arms are crossed low as if in self-protection.

■ Shoulders are hunched as if the person wants to shrink.

■ The person may step back for no reason.

■ Hand wringing reveals uncertainty.

■ Total stillness as if the person has been frozen literally in inaction.

■ The body curls into itself when seated or slumps.

■ Twining of legs is another form of self-comfort.

■ A shrug can look like a sign of hopelessness.

2 FACIAL EXPRESSIONS
■ Eyebrows are permanently raised as if anticipating criticism.

■ Features are constantly changing, revealing nervousness.

■ The chewing of the lower lip is like a child waiting to be scolded.

■ Blushing is a clear sign of embarrassment.

■ An overly apologetic look.

■ Eye contact is minimal as the person fears direct confrontation.

■ Eyes may close for a long time as if in disbelief or desperate to shut the other person out.

■ Lowered gaze suggest shame or guilt.

■ Eyes can blink frequently when the person is tense.

3 POSTURE
■ Round shoulders denote a shrinking violet.

■ A bent back can give the impression the person is in retreat or in hiding.

Using assertive body language

1 PHYSICAL DISTANCE
Be aware of how far and near you are standing to the other
person. When the person is standing too far, you should take
the initiative to move closer in subtle steps such as moving a
chair slowly away. Conversely, if the person is too close, don't
be worried about appearing rude if you move decisively away.

2 ROOM ARRANGEMENT
If you sit with someone diagonally across a desk, the exchange
is likely to be formal and sometimes confrontational. This may
be appropriate if you want to reprimand an employee and you
need to establish a certain distance. However if you are trying
to draw out a shy person or you want to congratulate a
co-worker on a job well done, it is more intimate to be seated
on a sofa without a table acting as a barrier.

3 SIGNS OF TENSION

Two sure signs of tension are when the back of the neck contracts and the shoulders hunch. To avoid these hints of tension, and therefore aggression, try dropping the shoulders and elongating the back of the neck.

4 TIRED SIGNS

You may appear tired and demoralized if you are sitting down and are hunched up. Try stretching your body up and opening up your chest. This will get more oxygen into your lungs and around your body and quickly make you feel more alert. Sit with your head up and shoulders back, and focus your eyes on the speaker, even if your head and shoulders feel tired.

how to practice assertive behavior

Using assertive body language continued

5 STANCE

Avoid leaning on one foot or leaning forward. Stand straight but leave your legs loose and flexible to show the audience that you are comfortable.

6 ARM GESTURES

Hand twisting, hair flicking, and face scratching detract from an otherwise confident delivery. Hand gesturing should be used with discretion to stress a particular point. To encourage diffident people to speak out, try open or outstretched palms.

7 EYE CONTACT

Light and intermittent eye contact can help to put other people at ease and show that you are acknowledging their presence. If you are pressing home a point, you might want to hold your stare on a person for longer than usual. Don't focus only on one person as it can be intimidating. Always make sure that you are keeping the whole audience with you by making contact with everyone. If you feel you are losing someone, perhaps because they are showing signs of boredom, sweep your eyes over them more frequently to be sure you get their attention back.

3

thinking assertively

thinking assertively

Understanding your rights

A first and vital step to thinking assertively is to be aware and understand that you are entitled to a fundamental set of rights. It is important to know these rights so that you can use them as a framework to decide whether other people are violating these rights or whether you in turn are disregarding other people's rights.

A basic set of rights were compiled by the United Nations in 1948 and set out as the Universal Declaration of Human Rights. The most pertinent points to the workplace are:

1 To be equal before the law regardless of race, color, sex, language, religion, political belief, or age.

2 The right to have opinions and express them without fear of aggression.

3 The right to work, to free choice of employment, to just and favorable conditions of work, and to protection against unemployment.

4 The right to equal pay for equal work.

5 The right to just and favorable remuneration, supplemented, if necessary, by other means of social protection.

6 The right to form and to join trade unions for the protection of his interests.

7 The right to rest and leisure, including reasonable limitation of working hours and periodic holidays with pay.

8 The right to a standard of living adequate for the health and well-being of himself and of his family, including food, clothing, housing, medical care, and necessary social services, and the right to security in the event of unemployment, sickness, disability, widowhood, old age, or other lack of livelihood in circumstances beyond his control.

9 Mothers and children are entitled to special care and assistance.

thinking assertively

Official and unofficial job rights

By law, private and state companies are obliged to write down basic job rights. Not all companies however are forced to develop additional rights not included in government law.

OFFICIAL RIGHTS INCLUDE:

1 A contract of employment

2 A comprehensive account of working conditions

3 Maternity leave policy

4 Measures for redundancy payment

Always check these four basic rights with the human resources department. If you are still unhappy about terms, check what is usual for your industry with your trade union.

UNOFFICIAL RIGHTS

This term covers areas that companies choose to take up as incentives for employees or for ethical reasons. There are also privileges that employees may have raised for themselves as part of their recruitment package. These include:

1 The right to study during company time whether by making up for lost time or by arranging to change salary or even to take a reduction in pay.

2 The right to a sabbatical after a certain period of time in employment.

3 The right to a job appraisal.

thinking assertively

Your employment contract

Some people prefer to have some aspects of their work duties deliberately left vague to give them more room for flexibility and initiative. For others though, many future disputes can be settled more easily and quickly if job descriptions and duties are clearly spelled out. Those with good negotiation skills may even request special sections to be included in a contract, though this is most likely to affect managers at the most senior level.

1 Are my daily duties clearly spelled out? Is there room for misinterpretation in some of the wording so that extra or unrelated work cannot be piled on without my consent?

2 Am I specified to work a certain amount of hours per week and to clock in and out at particular times?

3 Is there a provision to work from home if the situation arises?

4 Do I have one or more line managers? Who do I report directly to?

5 Who reports directly to me? How many people are under my supervision?

Your employment contract continued

6 Do I have a right to participate in any decisions that may affect my job?

7 Do I have a right to bonuses? How is the bonus worked out?

8 Do I have a right to make mistakes from time to time? Is there a system of warnings for these cases?

9 What room will I have to set my own agenda? How many people have to approve any new initiatives?

10 Do I have a right to a pay raise based on performance?
How often can I expect to get pay raises?

11 Is there a policy for the personal use of the Internet or the
phone during working hours?

12 Is there a sick-leave policy?

13 Is there a paid vacation time and can I take it when I choose
or is it scheduled by others?

Responsibilities

For a system of rights to work, you have to accept that other people have rights too, and your acceptance of rights entails that you have a set of responsibilities. These include:

1 To work the full hours you are paid for or to make provisions to compensate for any time taken off at work.

2 To meet deadlines agreed in advance.

3 To give reasonable and justified notice if any goals cannot be adequately met.

4 To take no more than the allocated holiday time.

5 To make requested changes to your work if agreed standards haven't been met.

6 If you are a manager, to give the appropriate supervision to employees if requested.

7 To admit to mistakes when they have been made and to rectify them.

8 To put the interests of the company before your own.

9 To follow the organization's rules and policies.

10 To work in harmony with colleagues in an atmosphere of trust and collaboration.

Behaviors and rights

1 ASSERTIVE

People who adopt assertive behavior understand their own rights as well as those of others. They feel easy about fighting for their entitlements when they are justified to do so. They can also stand back from a situation and appreciate that another person has equally valid claims. They seek a compromise that is fair to both parties.

2 AGGRESSIVE

Aggressive people have no problems understanding their rights and fighting their corner to make sure these are respected. However, they are far less adept at recognizing others' rights. They fail to see that ultimately, unless they respect other people's opinions and struggles, they can't expect others to take their demands seriously. By recognizing their own responsibilities in a bargain and by being more considerate about others, they may achieve their desired results far quicker than through unreasonable behavior.

3 PASSIVE

Passive people are frequently acknowledging other people's rights and giving in to their demands. But they don't seem to recognize that others should also respect their rights and wishes. Even when they are aware of their rights, they are too fearful to demand them and end up resigned and frustrated about having their needs ignored. Only when they believe that their rights are as important as everyone else's, can they expect consideration from others.

4 COMBINATION

People often exhibit a combination of behaviors in response to rights simply because some rights are more important to them than others. The right to flexible working hours, for example, may be more important to a worker with young children, while the right to join a labor union will be more important to someone else.

thinking assertively

Changing behavior patterns

People think they have a predominantly aggressive or passive nature, but behavior patterns are not set in stone. Once you have understood about your own rights and those of others, it is much easier to take the steps to make changes.

CHALLENGES TO CHANGE
It is important though to understand that there are stumbling blocks to modifying behavior so that you know what you are up against and you can react to it.

1 SAFETY
People strive for security and are reluctant to make any changes that will threaten this feeling of safety, in spite of the long-term benefits of change.

2 DENIAL
People will also go to great lengths to deny that a pattern of behavior has to change because it means facing painful realities and plucking up the courage and persistence to see a new plan of action through.

3 RESISTANCE
Inner negative thoughts about the potential harmful consequences of change can paralyze action especially if you have clung to your behavior patterns since childhood.

4 OTHER PEOPLE
When a work team has become accustomed to a set pattern of aggressive and passive behavior at the workplace, they will dislike any person who tries to change the balance of relations. They often have a vested interest in your remaining either passive or aggressive and may try to set you off course if they can. A passive person who becomes more confident and challenging may make some people feel they have lost their dominance. An aggressive person who decides to tone down their behavior will confuse people used to being ordered about. They may resent having to make their own decisions.

Changing behavior patterns continued

TIPS WHEN YOU SEEK CHANGE

1 Don't expect overnight results. Take pride in small steps. When you learn a new skill or habit, it usually takes about six weeks for it to really sink in.

2 Accept that you will sometimes fail and slip back. A passive person may find her new-found confidence intimidating. An aggressive person may lose patience with slow progress. Keep looking forward.

3 Keep reminding yourself of your rights. Thoughts will lead to action.

4 Make a list of small goals and check them off when you've achieved them. Then draw up a new list.

5 Repetition works. New challenges will soon become second nature.

6 Think of role models and try imitating some aspects of their behavior.

7 You have the option of not being assertive when incidents are too trivial to spend time on or maybe too dangerous not to walk away from.

8 Acknowledge small steps: these are what great strides are made from. Simply making a decision can be an enormous obstacle for some people. If you manage it, acknowledge it.

Reassessing beliefs

Now that you're committed to change, it is important to work on your self-image. A useful way to begin is to take a look at your belief system. Your beliefs about yourself and other people have a major influence on your behavior. You may think that other people share your beliefs, but this is often not the case. The way you look at the world may be completely different to the way others see it. You may be clinging on to a set of beliefs because it is safer and less trouble, but you do have the power to change your beliefs and consequently your behavior.

BELIEFS THAT ENCOURAGE AGGRESSIVE BEHAVIOR INCLUDE:

1 Only by being forceful can I get results.

2 I can't trust anyone else with a job.

3 I must always be in total control of my environment.

4 People must do as I direct.

BELIEFS THAT ENCOURAGE PASSIVE BEHAVIOR INCLUDE:

1 I'm not experienced enough for my opinions to count.

2 Others won't like me if I tell then what I really think.

3 I have to get this perfect or nobody will take me seriously.

BELIEFS AS OPPORTUNITIES:

1 I have a right to express opinions.

2 It doesn't matter if others disagree with me.

3 I have the power to change.

CHANGING BELIEFS

1 QUESTION THE PAST
People often cling to a set of beliefs that hark back a long way. They haven't modified them even though their circumstances may have changed dramatically. It's useful to question the past in light of your present life and to see your former opinions or other's thoughts about you are no longer relevant. Let go of antiquated beliefs.

2 LOOK AT THE EVIDENCE
You may have convinced yourself about certain aspects of your personality that you think you cannot change. What is the evidence for this belief in the last six months? Are you really correct in your assessment? Maybe you have had a mental block about a particular aspect and you can change.

3 TRY OUT DIFFERENT BELIEFS

It may be out of character but adopting a different belief for a short period is a way of testing out whether you get different results by trying a new course of action. You might get a surprisingly positive result and try acting out a new belief again until it becomes second nature.

4 SET YOURSELF GOALS

Drawing on your previous experience, set yourself future goals. These should be small and achievable. Set out short-term and long-term agendas. Question things, but don't get paralyzed by analysis: action is almost always more helpful than inaction or indecision.

thinking assertively
Combating negative thinking

Transforming a set of outdated or irrelevant beliefs takes you one step further toward assertive behavior, but what happens when strong negative feelings threaten to overturn or slow down any progress?

NEGATIVE FEELINGS THAT OVERCOME MOST PEOPLE INCLUDE:

1 Insecurity

2 Frustration

3 Anger

4 Guilt

5 Hurt

REACTIONS

PASSIVE people are likely to suppress these feelings or deny they even exist. The feelings won't go away and can lead to major stress.

AGGRESSIVE people won't hesitate in giving way to these feelings and letting others know about them. These outbursts may not necessarily solve their problems though, especially if others on the receiving end are shocked, intimidated, or annoyed by them. The results can be wholly negative.

REASONS FOR FEELINGS

It is easy to conclude that external situations and other people primarily affect your feelings but that puts you at the mercy of others to feel good or bad about yourself.

Could it be that past experiences are triggering off your present responses?

Could they be occurring out of force of habit?

Are they real responses to how you feel?

Combating negative thinking continued

Think about the last time you experienced negative feelings about a person, behavior, or situation, and try to answer the following questions honestly about it:

1 Are you exaggerating the event? Do others see the incident the way you do?

2 Are you jumping to conclusions and making sweeping statements?

3 Are you taking others' rights into accounts?

4 Are you standing up for your own needs and concerns?

5 Are you looking at the whole picture?

If you have answered mostly negatively, it may be that you are loading situations with a negative inner dialog. This means that before or during a given situation, your inner self is intervening with unproductive feelings that have predetermined the outcome from the outset.

You may have accepted the intrusion of this negative voice because it makes you feel safe. It can never surprise you. It may in fact have made you lazy.

By dismissing things offhand or not questioning the validity of negative comments, you don't work at improving yourself.

The good news for those who do want to change is that you have the power to fight this negative inner voice. Change is in your own hands.

Once you understand that you have the power to change, and accept that you want to change, you are well on the way to combating negativity.

thinking assertively

Thinking positive

The best way of combating negative inner voices is to create positive inner voices that will put up a fight and win.

ESTABLISHING POSITIVE POINTS

The first step toward developing a positive inner voice is to focus on positive things you have achieved in the past. The more you can pep yourself up with achievements, the less you will be prone to attack by self-doubt and the quicker you can train yourself to respond to negative thinking.

1 Jot down five things you've accomplished and explain why they are special to you. It doesn't matter if the incidents occurred a long time ago. Don't worry if they seem trivial or small because you were younger and less experienced. The main thing is that you try to capture the excitement and glow you felt for making them happen.

2 Conjure up images of one of these events before a difficult meeting or situation you may be dreading.

3 Make a list of three things you want to achieve in the next six months. Break them down into steps and check off any stages you have completed. Even if the ultimate goal seems a long way off, go back to the list to see how far you're advancing.

4 Think of incidents where your goal wasn't achieved but where you were proud of your effort. Sometimes you may do your best, and for reasons out of your control, you still don't win. Praise yourself for having giving it your all.

thinking assertively

Rehearsing positive inner voice

Before a potentially difficult situation, you may want to play out the possible scenarios that you are anticipating. That way you won't be caught saying to yourself things like "Now what do I say?" or "How can I make this better?"

1 CHOOSING THE RIGHT SITUATION
The first task is to choose the most appropriate situation to put your new assertive behavior into action. It is far better to start with a situation with which you are already comfortable. Tackling the difficult boss in day one is not advisable. An immediate failure will demotivate and stop the changing process on its tracks. Try weighing the pros and cons of two or three different situations and chose the one where you have the most to gain.

2 FOCUSING ON A PARTICULAR CASE
The more familiar you can become with one particular scenario, the more ready you will be to explore all the different angles and possible outcomes. Looking at a problem from all sides will help you to find a solution.

3 FEAR THE WORST

Play the situation in your head. Assume that what you are expecting could go wrong in the meeting does go wrong and that you respond with negative thoughts. Repeat the scene a couple of times until you are no longer frightened or surprised by the outcome. Were your negative reactions valid? Is there really no other way for you to act?

Example: A supervisor tells you that the workload has gone up so unexpectedly after the signing of two unexpected deals that you can't take the two weeks off you had planned. She tells you to change your plans and take the time off when the project is completed. You were really looking forward to the vacation but the boss has told you in a hurry. She doesn't seem to have time to discuss it further. You just stare back. "So that's settled" she says and walks off. You knew this was going to happen. You cancel your vacation.

Rehearsing positive inner voice continued

4 CHANGE THE SCRIPT

Hopefully you can distance yourself from the dreaded meeting enough to see that the outcome you most fear doesn't have to happen in reality. Play the scene again, this time pretending to be a person who reacts positively. It may seem out of character, and you may marvel at the daring involved. Play the scene again until you have internalized this positive behavior and are no longer fazed by it.

Example: The same scenario as before. You listen to the boss's demands but look unfazed. You take a deep breath before speaking. "I can see there's a lot of work to get through and I intend to do my best to finish the assignments that I have started on. I hear your suggestion of changing my holiday plans, but all the preparations have been made and my family is counting on me, I will be happy to tackle the projects when I am back."

5 ROLE PLAY

You may find it easier to test some of these scenarios out with a friend. In an interview scenario, for example, this can be a highly effective way of rehearsing possible responses. Alternatively, you can record a couple of speeches and play them back, underlining what parts you need to improve. Do you sound positive and upbeat? Are you using clear, jargon-free language to make your points logically? If you were listening to this speech, would you "buy" the message? If you are to give a presentation, for example, you can monitor timing, delivery of key points, verbal inflection, and so on to make your presentation more effective. Many public speakers—often the most effective— choose not to read speeches but simply rehearse all the relevant facts until they are confident of them and speak to their audience. This may be a good habit to adopt. Marshalling all the relevant facts in any situation will help you to respond effectively.

Playing out positive inner voice

You may have rehearsed the positive inner voice to perfection, but it is easy to be caught by surprise during a situation, especially if the other person or parties behave in a different way than you had anticipated. The following tips are aimed at helping to grapple with the unexpected:

1 WRITE DOWN OBJECTIVES
What do you expect to achieve from the meeting? What is the least you will be happy with? What won't you accept under any circumstances?

2 ASSESS RIGHTS
Go through what you reasonably have a right to and don't forget to see what the other party also has a right to. List them in points. That way you have an idea of the parameters available for negotiation.

3 PREPARE OPENING REMARKS

Try to get the first word in even if it is to recap why you are meeting and what you hope to get out of the meeting for both of you. If the other person tries to set the agenda before you, listen carefully and don't proceed until you're comfortable with the parameters the other person has set. If you aren't in agreement, here is your chance to spell out how you understand the purpose of the meeting. Setting this out from the beginning means any disagreement over the agenda does not cloud a productive outcome.

Playing out positive inner voice continued

4 BUY TIME

The other person may catch you by surprise. Buy yourself time by paraphrasing what the other person is telling you or by asking them to clarify their position. Try phrases like: "So what you're saying is..." or "Would you like to explain further?"

5 PAUSE

Don't feel rushed into making an immediate response. Take a deep breath to help you relax. Use the time to clear your head and gather your thoughts together for the next point before you continue.

6 LOOK CALM
Try not to look surprised. You can't always be ready for a change of response, but you can at least brace yourself for being caught unaware.

7 POSTPONE OUTCOME
If you are really stuck, ask for more time. Don't let the other person push toward a resolution then and there if you are not happy about it. Try a phrase like "Thanks for letting me know your position. I would like time to give it my full consideration and will get back to you shortly."

Playing back positive inner voice

Sometimes, in spite of the best intentions, you manage to slip back into old habits and negative thoughts take over, particularly when a meeting hasn't gone as planned or you forgot everything you had rehearsed. It is essential to review the incident in a positive light.

1 EXAGGERATE FOR EFFECT
After an unsatisfactory meeting, you may be prone to playing back the meeting, highlighting the negative aspects until you've blown them out of all proportion. You can use this exaggeration for effect if it draws attention to the fact that you are overreacting. Repeat the scene in your head until it becomes less shocking. Build up the worst possible case scenario only to deflate it.

2 ACCEPT IMPERFECTION
You may be new to this soul searching and need more practice. Accept that you can't be perfect and that you will do better next time. The only way to improve is practice. In time, you will get more effective, and the whole process will become first familiar, and then second nature.

3 LEARN FROM FAILURE
Use the failure as a lesson. Play back the scene the way you would ideally like to behave. Examine where you were caught out. Write any obvious errors in strategies down. It will help you not to repeat these next time.

4 SAVOR SUCCESS
If the meeting has gone well, it's easy to overlook it as you prepare for the next stage. Take some time to replay the successful incident and enjoy it.

5 CHALLENGE YOURSELF
The small steps are fine but don't stop there. If you've honed a few skills during a meeting, this may be the time to consider whether the next target is that difficult boss.

6 PRAISE YOURSELF
Finally, don't forget to give yourself a good pat in the back for the progress you have made.

Visualizing positive thoughts

Speaking positively to yourself is one part of thinking positively. Visualizing positive images or scenes of yourself in given situations will also help you develop a positive aura. If you have trouble projecting an image of yourself, try the following relaxation exercises:

1 Find a quiet room or space. Sit down in a comfortable chair or lie down on the ground. Close your eyes, count to ten and feel your body go loose.

2 Try to stretch the body as long as you can.

3 Think of yourself in one of your favorite settings. Imagine you are there: the beach, a tennis court, in a forest. Visualization in this way leads to mental calm and stimulates positive thoughts. It slows the heart rate slightly, which will make you feel calmer and more relaxed.

VISUALIZING POSITIVE WORK IMAGES
When you have become more adept at relaxing, transfer the positive images of recreation time to an office environment.

1 Have a mental image of yourself leaving a room having achieved exactly what you wanted.

2 Visualize yourself looking relaxed as you put across your thoughts.

3 Watch other people paying close attention to you.

4 Picture yourself listening to others and showing them you are listening.

5 Watch people nod their heads in disagreement without taking it as a personal slight on you. They are merely expressing a different opinion.

6 Imagine people's faces changing expressions as they show they can change their opinions. This may be from disbelief to belief, from incomprehension to understanding, or from distrust to acceptance.

VISUALS AND AFFIRMATIONS
To further ingrain a positive outlook try and match some of your inner positive talk with the positive images of yourself:

1 Jot down positive words about yourself and try to find visual images that reinforce the feelings.

2 Make a list of positive affirmations. Examples are "I have the right to say no," "I can ask my boss an awkward question without the fear of looking ridiculous," "I can speak up at a meeting with lots of people," "I can remain calm even when I feel very angry." To all these affirmations, create a small visual story that illustrates them.

Visualizing positive thoughts continued

FIVE QUICK STEPS TO AFFIRMATIVE THINKING

1 RIGHTS
Accept that you have the right to change, to be positive, and to stand up for yourself.

2 POSITIVE INNER VOICE
Give yourself positive pep talks. The negative inner voice will resist, but with practice the positive inner voice will win.

3 POSITIVE VISUALIZATION
Create images of your positive actions to reinforce your positive inner voice.

4 POSITIVE AFFIRMATION
Confirm the progress made by your inner voice and
visualization with positive statements like "I can confront this
difficult person in a dignified manner that won't hurt me" or
"It's in my power to secure this deal."

5 POSITIVE RESULTS
Savor your successes and let these feed your positive inner
voice. Success that is achieved against the odds is worth
taking time to enjoy. Replay it in your mind, and log it as
something to savor in more difficult situations in the future.

4

assertiveness
in specific situations

Handling aggressive behavior

One of the biggest tests to assertiveness is confronting aggressive behavior which can take various forms: personal attacks, angry outbursts, sarcasm, put-downs, and deliberate indifference.

EFFECTS ON YOU:
People use aggressive behavior to influence an outcome. They do this by trying to incite an emotional reaction that takes you by surprise and prevents you from looking at the situation objectively, weighing the facts and reaching a decision.

1 It is very easy to counter an attack with anger or exasperation. This loss of control lessens the impact of any valid content you may be discussing.

2 You may also withdraw from any intended plan of action or at least delay the process, which weakens your position. You may fear encouraging anger if you retaliate, yet you know that this is likely if you delay or prevaricate.

At the heart of your retreat to aggressive and passive responses are negative inner thoughts caused by anger, embarrassment, hurt, fear, and frustration. This is what you should do:

HOW TO RESPOND ASSERTIVELY IN SEVEN STEPS:

1 SLOW DOWN
The aggressive person is trying to catch you by surprise or elicit a quick response from you. It is best to buy some time by resorting to questions that force the aggressor to repeat himself or to explain herself more fully. That way you shift the exchange to facts and steer away from emotions that can lead you to lose the initiative.

2 ACKNOWLEDGE
Let the aggressor know that you have understood her grievances. It doesn't mean you agree. It merely shows you are prepared to listen. Inviting further comment may disarm or shock the aggressor—she's not used to having people actually listen—and may mean that you do, in fact, have a more productive discussion.

Handling aggressive behavior continued

3 EXPRESS VIEW
Let the aggressor know your position. State your viewpoint clearly. Use phrases such as "My understanding of the situation is ..." and "That is why I have acted in this way."

4 PARAPHRASE
If the aggressive behavior continues, you can retaliate with repetition of your own: paraphrase her grievances and repeat your point of view. "I understand that you are unhappy about xxx, but my understanding of the situation is different, hence my actions."

5 SUGGEST SOLUTIONS
Provide some alternatives and implicate her in the decision. "It seems we have a few choices. What do you think?" "I'm sure that one of these options will satisfy everybody's concerns." Express your confidence that there will be a positive outcome.

6 POSTPONE RESOLUTION
In some cases, the aggressor won't alter her course. Don't walk away as that is allowing emotions to take over your decision making. If you are going to cut off interaction, let the person know. "I see we can't come to a conclusion. I suggest we come back to it when you have calmed down." This allows you to have the last say and puts you in control. The attempts to force you into an emotional response have failed.

7 FOLLOW THROUGH
The corollary to postponing resolution, however, is that you must follow through. Set up a time when everyone has calmed down to talk again.

Handling passive behavior

Nonassertive behavior also poses challenges to assertiveness because it also tries to influence behavior by inciting emotions like guilt, frustration, anger, pity, and indecision.

EFFECTS ON YOU:

1 A nonassertive response to a new plan you announce can act as a most effective obstacle to your initiatives. The lack of energy and enthusiasm inherent in passive behavior can be infectious. You can feel listless. Maybe you'll start questioning the plan. You may retreat into inaction or doubt the effectiveness of the plan.

2 You can also react to the indifference of a nonassertive response with anger. Why isn't the person responding more positively? Why can't you read what the person really thinks of the project? If you express frustration and still elicit no positive response, you will come across as unreasonable and authoritative.

HOW TO RESPOND ASSERTIVELY IN SIX STEPS:

1 QUESTION
Passive people can use lack of communication as a weapon.
Don't let them remain silent. Ask open-ended questions and
make sure you listen if answers are forthcoming.

2 QUESTION AGAIN
Nonassertive people are adept at deflecting opportunities
to speak out that demand them to take a stance. Don't be
satisfied with the first answers. Keep probing and continue to
ask open questions such as "why," "when," and "how," rather
than closed questions, which can only be answered with a
"yes" or "no."

Handling passive behavior continued

3 PARAPHRASE
By replaying their comments back to them in your own words
you are not only showing them that you are listening, you are
also checking that they agree with the assessment. That way
they have less power to keep you in doubt.

4 QUESTION AGAIN
You can't ask passive people enough times for input as they
are not going to offer solutions. This is their chance to suggest
a way to forward themselves.

Keep asking open questions (questions that generally begin
with "how," "why," "what," "when," and similar words) and
avoid trying to suggest answers yourself. A passive person
may pick up on the answer he suspects you want to hear,
which is going to help no one.

5 SUGGEST SOLUTIONS
In the most stubborn cases, responses will still be monosyllabic
or unhelpful. As with aggressive people, you can give them a
choice to keep them involved. It may be that their feeling of
being overlooked in the past has encouraged their passivity.

6 QUESTION
By now, you must know that handing them the initiative is
one of your main objectives. Ask them to decide which of the
solutions they are happy with or if they can come up with an
alternative. In the case of the most taciturn, give them a time
frame to come up with their answer. By the end of the
exchange, you should feel that you have recovered the
initiative and have the upper hand.

Negotiating conflicting needs

Assertiveness is vital for successfully managing an acceptable outcome from a situation where two or more people have different and often clashing needs. These are some typical ways in which people try to successfully resolve conflicting needs:

1 ASSERTIVE-ASSERTIVE
When both parties lay out honestly their needs and yet remain respectful of the other's rights, then a real dialogue can ensue. Even if some sort of compromise has to be made, at least both parties leave the exchange feeling that they have dealt with the conflict in the most positive way possible.

2 AGGRESSIVE-AGGRESSIVE
This exchange occurs when both parties believe the only solution is for one party to win at the expense of the other. At the root of this method is the unwillingness for both people to recognize the other's rights.

3 AGGRESSIVE-PASSIVE
This is the most typical exchange as it tends to occur
between bosses and subordinates where the higher ranked
manager uses rank and seniority to steer the outcome.
Employees may accept that the boss will always have the
ultimate say, but the residues of resentment in these
exchanges are not optimal. It is also unhelpful for a boss
to constantly pull rank to push through unpopular or
ineffective solutions.

4 PASSIVE-PASSIVE
When employees have similar positions, this type of exchange
is more frequent. Both parties tend to overlook their own rights
and needs for different reasons. Each is so concerned that they
don't appear as the aggressor or the bully that the outcome
can end up unsatisfactory for both. Neither side has expressed
their real needs, so there are no grounds for negotiation.

Negotiating needs assertively

1 ESTABLISH YOUR POSITION
To establish any ground rules, both parties have to be open about their needs. State clearly your ideal scenario.

2 ESTABLISH THEIR POSITION
Invite the other person to describe his ideal outcome. If he is reluctant to come out with a clear statement, probe with a few questions and if necessary, paraphrase his needs.

3 ACCEPT NEEDS
Let the person know you understand his needs and ask them whether they understand yours. This confirms that you are both in agreement about the parameters for the negotiation.

4 OFFER SUGGESTIONS
It is best to have drawn up a few potential scenarios before the meeting. That way you will know exactly the advantages and disadvantages of each alternative and be aware of which will work best for you.

5 BE OPEN TO SUGGESTION
You may also be surprised by an alternative you haven't thought of. Listen carefully to the feedback.

6 BARGAIN
Identify the good and bad points with each solution and suggest that you both make some compromises.

7 ACCEPT COMPROMISE
Sometimes the outcome won't match your ideal scenario. Be satisfied that you dealt with the negotiations without treading on anyone's toes and with no regrets.

8 MOVE ON
Once a compromise has been reached, accept it, and move on rather than dwell on what might have been. A decision taken is better than one not taken, so move forward.

Making requests

Making requests of other people at work is a commonplace and necessary activity, so why do some people find it difficult to ask people to do something for them? Moreover, why do others have no problem asking but don't get results?

ASSERTIVE BEHAVIOR: ATTITUDE TO REQUESTS

1 People have the right to make requests.

2 People have a right to refuse requests.

ASSERTIVE BEHAVIOR: OUTCOME

1 People are happy to accept a request because they know exactly where they stand.

2 People feel they have a choice in accepting a request so are more willing to acquiesce.

3 People feel valued and respected.

AGGRESSIVE BEHAVIOR: ATTITUDE TO REQUESTS

1 My demands are more important than others are.

2 It is my right to demand requests from people.

3 If my requests are turned down, it's an affront to my authority. What I say goes, and anyone who does not agree with this and acts accordingly is undermining my position.

Making requests continued

AGGRESSIVE BEHAVIOR: OUTCOME

1 People feel put upon by aggressive demands and will refuse the request in rebellion.

2 If they feel forced to accept, they will do the job grudgingly.

3 People won't volunteer to help in the future. There is no incentive for goodwill when those making requests take others for granted.

PASSIVE BEHAVIOR: ATTITUDE TO REQUESTS

1 Other people's demands take priority.

2 If people refuse to help me, it shows they don't like me.

3 Asking for things is a sign of weakness.

PASSIVE BEHAVIOR: OUTCOME

1 Passive people will take longer to get projects done because they don't manage to build a supportive team.

2 They make demands after a lot of apologizing. This is frustrating for people who have agreed to help.

Making requests continued

TIPS FOR MAKING REQUESTS ASSERTIVELY

1 DON'T TAKE REFUSAL PERSONALLY
You have nothing to lose asking others for help. That is the
nature of office life. If someone turns your request down, it
doesn't mean they don't like you. Nor does it mean she can't
help you in the future. They are simply not able to accept on
this occasion.

2 KEEP IT BRIEF AND SUCCINCT
There's nothing worse than veering off the point when the
person being asked a favor can guess that the speaker is
coming around to making a request. This makes her feel
manipulated. It's far better to be direct. Explain your needs
and set a time frame.

3 AVOID FLATTERY
Praising a colleague can come across as suspicious, uncalled
for, and patronizing.

4 DON'T APOLOGIZE
You don't have to be sorry or make a hundred excuses for
making the request. Apologizing in advance trivializes the
request. If you make the request seriously enough and
transmit the fact that it needs to be taken seriously, the
chance that the other person will give the request its due
consideration is greater. Keep reminding yourself that
reasonable requests such as this one deserve reasonable
responses and act accordingly.

Making requests continued

5 OFFER ALTERNATIVES
Sometimes offering a co-worker a menu of requests to pick from makes them feel less put upon. It also makes them feel that they have more choices.

6 BROKEN RECORD
This method of repeating yourself like a broken record, demands persistence and a thick skin, but it can be very effective against people who can't match your persistence.

7 ACCEPT "NO" WITH GRACE
Persistence is a virtue in business but harassing colleagues with extra pleas for help can become bullying. Your fellow workers and subordinates have rights, and one of those is the right to say "no."

FIVE SHORTCUTS TO ASKING FOR WHAT YOU WANT

1 Address the person by their name.

2 Express your need.

3 Explain why you need to do it.

4 Inform when you need it done.

5 End with a "thank you." Whereas "please" gives the person the chance to say "no," "thank you" is more forceful. It assumes that the other person will do what you have asked.

Chairing meetings

Why is it essential to be assertive if you are chairing a meeting?

1 Few tasks will test your leadership more than trying to supervise a room of up to a dozen people (the maximum number for a manageable meeting).

2 Meetings are held to introduce new agendas, debate pressing issues, and inspire team spirit. If unsuccessful, this will reflect badly on managers and create more problems.

3 Some team members are more reluctant to share opinions with a group than on a one-to-one meeting. It is up to the manager to draw these people out for an effective outcome.

4 If you are aggressive, the team will view the meeting more as a summons where they are being given orders and no opportunity for contributions. If you are passive, they will feel you have no direction.

KEEP ALERT FOR:

1

Problem: The person who rambles on and on.

Solution: Signal that you are listening and then interrupt by calling the person's name. Try a phrase like "That is interesting, and we can bring that point up later. Can we please turn to item x" or a simple "Thank you. I must stop you there."

2

Problem: The silent person.

Solution: Don't be afraid to ask them an open question ("how?" "why?" or "when?"). Make sure you go around the table with questions so no one feels picked on. Show you are listening to them. This is not the same as agreeing with them.

3

Problem: An argument arises from two clashing personalities.

Solution: Don't come down on one side. Ask them how their dispute is contributing to the main items on the agenda and swiftly move on.

Chairing meetings continued

SOME TIPS FOR SMOOTH MEETINGS:

1 Send an email/memo outlining the reasons for the meeting in advance. Include the names of people attending so that no one is caught by surprise. If you are sending any accompanying literature, keep it short and request all attendees to read it before the meeting.

2 Begin the meeting with a quick summary of the goals of the meeting and the three to five points to discuss. Let them know the amount of time you expect to spend on each item.

3 Try to sum up any points, even if there is no consensus, for each item discussed.

4 When you interrupt, use first names, it commands more attention.

5 Don't shout, even if others are shouting.

6 End on a positive note. Paraphrase the main points, thank members for attending, and follow up the results and any pending, unresolved issues with an email or a memo. Depending on the culture in your organization, personally thanking people by telephone may help people to keep feeling positive about outcomes.

Contributing to meetings

Many people find meetings a frustrating process because they either find they never have enough time to state their views or they feel intimidated to express themselves in a large group. A failure by the chair to explain the main reason for the meeting also encourages negative attitudes toward meetings. There are several ways of taking a proactive stance to meetings that will benefit you and other participants.

REMEMBER RESPONSIBILITIES

1 As a member of the team invited to a meeting, remember the responsibilities of the chair toward you and other particpants, and your responsibilities as an attendee.

2 If you don't know the main objectives of the meeting, don't be afraid to ask. You may even want to suggest to the chair that you are eager to raise a point that you consider to be missing from the agenda.

3 A lot of meetings drag on especially if they have no relevance to your department. You have a right to decline joining a meeting if you can justify that it really is inappropriate. Make sure, however, that you have very good reasons.

4 You have a right to know how long the meeting will last.

5 Once you've accepted to join, you have every right to contribute and disagree with some of the measures that the meeting may be trying to push through. There is no point in being there if your role is simply to be a "yes" man whose presence and aquiescence will be used in a numbers game ("90 percent of people at the meeting agreed…," for example).

Contributing to meetings continued

FOCUS ON POSITIVE INNER THOUGHTS

1 It may seem intimidating to be sitting around a table with the most senior members of the company, but remember you have been asked to attend for a reason, and they will expect to hear your views. No one will judge you for speaking out.

2 If you don't understand a point, don't be afraid to ask for clarification. If you don't understand, it's likely that others won't either.

3 Remind yourself how frustrated you can feel after a lousy meeting where you wish you had spoken out or that you had challenged others on an item you disagreed on. Be determined not to repeat that mistake.

4 Don't think you'll be judged personally if you express differences with the majority.

5 Look all members in the eye when you are talking or listening. This shows you are actively participating.

6 Keep your body language neutral. You do not want to be seen as taking sides, but you do want to be seen as being open to all ideas and information and a frank and formal discussion of ideas. If your body language starts to slip from neutral you may come over as too formal or too casual, and as someone who is not giving the proceedings the attention and thought they deserve.

Contributing to meetings continued

TRAPS TO AVOID

1 Know the limitations of a meeting. If you have made a point, don't belabor it. There is nothing worse than the person who hijacks a meeting to express his pet subject that interrupts the main concerns of the meeting.

2 Don't look away from the person who you are disagreeing with. Treat others with respect.

3 Interruptions are valid to correct a speaker who has made a glaring error, but they come across as pedantic if they are over minor matters.

4 Remember that the meeting is not about you. Acknowledge that everyone has a right to be heard and listen attentively. Try to reach an agreement but be pragmatic if this is impossible.

Making presentations

A good presentation can help you shine and help to further your goals; however, a poor one can undermine your ideas, no matter how valid, and your authority. Assertive skills like body language and voice quality will help to ensure a successful presentation:

1 Keep your delivery on the slow side. Rattling through will make it seem as if you want to get the report over with, and your statements will lose their force.

2 Use short phrases and sentences.

3 All attention will be on your body language, so keep an upright posture, keep the neck upright, stand firm, and don't fidget with your arms unless it is to make a firm point.

4 Try to focus on certain people in different parts of the room. It's encouraging to catch the eye of particularly attentive people from time to time as they will help you feel that what you are saying is important. Keep sweeping your gaze across the room at regular intervals.

5 Don't read from written notes as this will keep your head down and your delivery stilted. By all means, use notes as references, but try to use everyday, informal conversation as much as possible. Reading a prepared script makes your delivery flat and may bore your audience.

Making presentations continued

6 Make sure any computers or overhead projectors that you are using for visual aids work before you make your presentation. There is nothing more off-putting than a speaker fidgeting with machines when he is supposed to be speaking.

7 Keep your audience involved with hypothetical questions, which you can come back to for discussion.

8 Dress appropriately for the type of audience you are expecting, even if your normal style is different. Make sure you feel comfortable, so wear the clothes at least once beforehand. Unbutton your jacket so that you can move freely and extend your hand or arm for emphasis. Make sure your shoes are comfortable, especially if you are going to be moving around.

9 End on a positive note and invite questions from the floor.

10 Take notes during questions and don't worry about taking a little time to answer.

11 If you are confused by a question that seems to be more of a statement, paraphrase what you think the question is.

12 Don't answer a question if you don't know the answer. If there is a valid question that you can't answer, make detailed notes, and ask if someone can get back to them. For example, "I'd like to ask my IT manager to respond to that" or "That's one for my marketing manager. Can I ask him to call you?"

5

being assertive
with subordinates

being assertive with subordinates

Stating your views

Different viewpoints are inevitable at work and they can be expressed and interpreted in three different ways:

ASSERTIVE BEHAVIOR: THE SIGNS

1 Putting your views across without fear of how this will affect you personally.

2 Listening to other people's views.

3 Agreeing to disagree on certain points.

4 Asking questions. Trying to find answers that suit both parties.

ASSERTIVE BEHAVIOR: THE REASONING

1 Different opinions are useful.

2 Everyone has a right to an opinion.

3 One of my responsibilities is to take others into account.

ASSERTIVE BEHAVIOR: THE OUTCOME

1 A potential solution that keeps both parties relatively happy has been negotiated. Nobody feels she has lost the battle.

2 Everyone knows and understands the ground rules, so they have a basis for negotiation in the future.

Stating your views continued

AGGRESSIVE BEHAVIOR: THE SIGNS

1 Denies the other's viewpoint.

2 All debates must end in victory for one party and loss for the other.

3 Unpleasant working atmosphere: shouting, put-downs, frequent interruptions.

AGGRESSIVE BEHAVIOR: THE REASONING

1 In business, all solutions are clear-cut.

2 Give in an inch, and the enemy will walk all over you.

3 How dare subordinates question me?

AGGRESSIVE BEHAVIOR: THE OUTCOME

1 Issues and facts are swallowed up by emotions. There is no resolution to a situation.

2 People resent giving in and seek future non-cooperation.

Stating your views continued

PASSIVE BEHAVIOR: THE SIGNS

1 Avoids open conflict.

2 Glosses over differences.

3 Any disagreement is tentative: "I'm not sure that I'm in agreement with that."

PASSIVE BEHAVIOR: THE REASONING

1 Disagreement disturbs harmony at work.

2 Conflict is risky: it could lead to ridicule or losing my job.

3 It's my responsibility to follow whatever's decided at the senior management level.

4 Someone else will pick up on the difficulties.

PASSIVE BEHAVIOR: THE OUTCOME

1 Important issues are not raised and can't be taken into account.

2 Resentment brews inside the passive person.

3 There is no resolution.

How to state views assertively

1 DISTINGUISH FACTS
Use "I" statements to underline the difference between your thoughts and the facts.

2 ACKNOWLEDGE
Show that you understand the other person's point of view by paraphrasing it: "I understand that what you are saying is...." This demonstrates that you are actively listening.

3 EXPLAIN
Justify your view. Don't expect people to understand, explain your objectives. Don't expect subordinates to guess what you want.

4 BALANCE
State clearly the main positions of both viewpoints and emphasize the grounds for agreement. "I see what you mean by x but I don't agree with y."

How to disagree

Stating your views will sometimes inevitably lead to disagreement. How do you disagree without getting upset or falling out with the other person?

1 AFFIRM

The more natural response to a statement we disagree with is to say "no" immediately. For instance, if a colleague asks you if you agree with his decision to hire his favorite candidate for a job and you are not in agreement, you may instinctively say "no." But try starting with a "yes." It can be disarming for the person asking.

2 ACKNOWLEDGE

This is a softening tactic whereby you show you are taking his opinion into account. "Yes, I understand why you think x is a suitable candidate."

3 EXPLAIN

Then state your view: You don't have to use the words "but" or "however" as they sound negative. Simply come out with your opinion. "The reasons I think he may not be the right candidate are the following." By explaining, you are not dismissing his comment or undermining him.

4 DISAGREE

Come to a firm conclusion. The word "so" is very powerful as it sounds like you have followed a logical argument to its inevitable conclusion. "So I think the candidate would not be appropriate for the job."

5 COMPROMISE

If the person you are disagreeing with is aggressive and insists on his decision, you have the option of offering a couple of alternatives: "Can you reconsider the other two shortlisted candidates?" You are not committing yourself to a final decision but giving the other person another chance to express an opinion. This is a win-win situation.

being assertive with subordinates

Giving criticism

Why are bosses particularly bad at handing criticism? This is true, mainly because so many people take criticism about a job as personal. Also, more often than not, criticism carries negative, destructive connotations rather than constructive, positive associations aimed at helping future behavior. There are two instinctive responses by bosses faced with giving criticism:

1 AGGRESSIVE DELIVERY STYLE
Bosses will raise the problem at an inappropriate time, perhaps in front of other people. They will be angry and frustrated, deliver the criticism quickly, and then walk out, leaving the recipient with no time to respond or to ask any questions.

2 PASSIVE DELIVERY STYLE
Bosses will avoid bringing up the subject or procrastinate while the problem gets worse. When they do raise it, it will be tentative and lack clarity. This is open to confusion and misinterpretation on the one hand, and to indifference on the other.

OUTCOME IN BOTH CASES

1 The recipient is given no clear explanation as to what particular aspect of her job needs improving.

2 The recipient has no opportunity to participate in the process of improvement. The passive boss is uncomfortable with dwelling on the criticism so would rather avoid a follow-up discussion while the aggressive boss is only interested in her own viewpoint.

3 Resignation or rebellion are likely results. The boss has not advanced her objective to change behavior. By not allowing a frank discussion of what needs to be changed and the most effective ways of doing it, stagnation sets in, which is in no one's interest, including the organization as a whole.

Giving criticism continued

WHAT YOU SHOULD DO

1 AGGRESSIVE
You have a right to expect improvements in particular tasks, but not to be rude to employees. Bettering the performance in her department is no excuse to put people down or make them feel inferior. Underperformance should have no relationship to personality issues.

2 PASSIVE
It is your responsibility to make sure that members of your team improve their performance when necessary. Pointing out these areas of concern to employees is part and parcel of the job. Everyone's job requires monitoring from time to time and feedback, positive and negative, is not only natural, but also helpful to others. Adopting behavior patterns that don't allow you to do this is unhelpful and failing in your responsibilities as a manager.

TIPS FOR HANDING CRITICISM

1 STICK TO FACTS

The most sensitive aspect of handing criticism is keeping observations from sounding like personal attacks. Bosses will get far better results if they try to quantify exactly what aspects of behavior need changing. Write them down and try and provide examples.

For instance, don't use sarcasm to demand better time keeping. A phrase like "Have you ever arrived on time?" or "What's your excuse this time?" will just get the latecomer's back up. The insinuation is that you have already made up your mind about his lateness. Instead, try sounding concerned "I notice you haven't been able to make it on time this week. Is there a problem?" If the lack of punctuality continues, you could appeal to the effect of the lateness on other people. "The project is suffering by your not being here with the rest of the team." Above all, be specific. "I expect you to be here by x" is more helpful than "Don't arrive late again."

Giving criticism continued

2 EXPLAIN
It seems very simple, but many bosses dish out criticism without putting their comments into context. If you put the criticism into a logical context, the recipient will be far more aware of the consequences of his actions. Explain that a particular department goal is not being met and then suggest that the person's behavior or way of operating may be one of the causes. For instance: "The report is almost ready to send to the client but there are some vital numbers missing. Could you verify these and then send the completed version to the illustrators?" The recipient sees a cause and effect and is motivated to complete the task.

3 CONSIDER IN CONTEXT
Include positives: "I realize that a certain project required a lot of your time, but it would have been more helpful if you had warned me that a major aspect of your job was not being completed effectively because of that." This gives a context to any discussion.

4 INVITE PARTICIPATION

Allow the person receiving the criticism to comment on the fairness or otherwise of your comments. "Do you think this is fair?" or "Does this come as a surprise?" are straightforward enough openings and appear nonjudgmental on your part. Maybe you don't see the complete picture, or some vital information may have been kept away from you. Or perhaps the employee was unaware of the problem because of lack of previous supervision or information. Don't assume the other person is aware of the problem. Getting agreement with the criticism is a helpful way of establishing that both parties understand the nature of the problem and know the way forward.

5 SUMMARIZE

Paraphrasing the exchange and going through the points discussed and the agreed plan of action helps to create the impression that both parties have moved forward. Try a phrase like "So we agree that for next time...?" It also makes it clear that the employee understands the nature of the criticism and gives him the last chance to raise any objections.

Giving praise

Handing criticism, however difficult for some managers, is more commonplace than giving praise. There are several reasons for this:

1 Giving praise is seen as soft in many traditional companies. Employees might misinterpret praise as a sign of weakness.

2 Subordinates are expected to perform, that is their responsibility. They don't need praise. They are only doing their job.

3 Praise does not have the same definite outcome (i.e., a change in behavior) as criticism.

4 Praise can be interpreted as a bribe.

5 It can be awkward to give praise when the recipient doesn't know how to respond or fails to appreciate it.

AGGRESSIVE

Insensitive bosses may turn genuine praise into negative criticism. "It's taken long enough to produce those figures but at least we've got them now. Will you be faster next time?" or "This is good. Did you really do this on your own? It's not at all like your usual work."

PASSIVE

Nonassertive bosses may be hesitant and unclear. "The way you handled the customer yesterday. Er, it seemed to do the trick. They won't bother us again. What I mean is that you seemed to cope well...."

Or they may use praise to put the department down. "The way you handled that customer was rather good. It's a shame it doesn't happen more often in the department."

Giving praise continued

TIPS FOR GIVING PRAISE ASSERTIVELY:

1 Be clear and focus on the behavior. Gushing can appear contrived or insincere. Ramble too long and the message will be obscured.

2 Make the criticism as quickly after the event as possible.

3 Encourage as well as praise. "Keep up the good work" is simple but effective.

4 Highlight a fact to show you have really taken notice. "I especially liked the section on xxx" before delivering aspects that need improvement.

5 Keep eye contact and try a smile to show you appreciate the particular incident or behavior.

6 Encourage the person if you notice that they have made an effort to change their behavior.

Managing a downsizing

One of the worst possible scenarios for managers is to let staff go when a company downsizes. That's why some companies hire a manager specifically for the task. Assertive behavior facilitates the process. These are some tips:

1 RECOGNIZE RESPONSIBILITIES
You can behave more assertively if you remember that you are responsible for both the economic well-being of the company and the well-being of the staff. When reducing staff, the two responsibilities appear to contradict each other. It is your duty to make sure the process goes as smoothly as possible.

2 BE DISCRETE
Do not tell any member of staff, however trusted, the news of a redundancy before you tell the people involved. Avoid the temptation of sharing the burden by offloading the news.

3 ARRANGE A MEETING AS EARLY AS POSSIBLE
Arrange to talk in private toward the end of the day so the worker can go home to reflect on the news. If you expect people to leave immediately, tell them in the morning to give them the rest of the day to clear their desks.

4 BE DIRECT
A preamble about the state of the economy or the company's problems is unhelpful. Have a phrase ready to lead up to the news, such as "We have made the decision to downsize."

5 ACKNOWLEDGE
Most people will respond passively or aggressively as these are the most spontaneous reactions to bad news. Typical reactions are to go silent, burst into tears, or get very angry. They may blame you. Don't take it personally. Acknowledge how they are feeling by playing back some of their responses.

6 DON'T APOLOGIZE
Apologies can come across as contrived or as a sign of guilt.

7 INFORM STAFF
Once the people who are going have been informed, spell the facts out to stop unnecessary rumors, pacify any fearful staff, and give the impression that the process is under control.

Handling personal issues

There are four personal issues that most managers dread dealing with:

1 SEXUAL BEHAVIOR
Problem: Office romances should be outside a manager's remit until it starts affecting the working environment. For instance, two members of the staff who had an affair that ended badly can cause friction in a team if they have to continue working together but fail to communicate or, if they do, are hostile to each other.

Solution: Don't pussy-foot around the issue. Arrange separate conversations with the two staff members and explain out front why their private relationship is affecting the business. Let them know that your main concern is that their behavior toward each other should not infringe on the rest of the team.

2 EXCESSIVE ALCOHOL

Problem: Drinking after work is an acceptable form of corporate bonding and is even encouraged in many companies by the hosting of frequent drinks, outings, or parties. Difficulties arise when people drink excessively and either fail to turn up to work the next day or, if they do, to perform inadequately. Also, if they get very drunk in a company activity, they can turn aggressive, even nasty with co-workers.

Solution: Be direct with the person and focus on the excessive drinking activity. Allow him to talk about the problem. If the response is either passive like a complete denial or aggressive like an angry outburst, then it is your duty to tell him that you are handing the matter over to human resources. Remain matter of fact and avoid any judgments, but make certain that the person understands the seriousness of the situation.

Handling personal issues continued

3 BODY ODOR

Problem: A lack of personal hygiene is possibly the most difficult problem to confront as it is most difficult to link the problem with behavior or an activity.

Solution: It is far easier to approach a person of the same sex with the problem. If the person is of the opposite sex, you may be better off delegating the matter to a close colleague of the opposite sex. Try the surprised approach: "I'm sure this doesn't happen very often but I've noticed in the last few days..." This may not sound assertive because it is not totally direct (the person may have had the problem for longer). But you are still letting the offending person know of the problem while allowing her to save face with the suggestion that it may be a temporary problem. Move swiftly on to another topic to show you are not embarrassed about bringing the topic up.

4 SHOULDER TO CRY ON
Problem: A member of the staff is having a bad time personally, perhaps he is going through a messy divorce. The trouble is that not only is this affecting his own work, but in being tearful or angry about the situation he is affecting those around him. Fellow workers might be genuinely sympathetic, but the office environment cannot be used as a counseling service.

Solution: Offer a short but reasonable leave of absence while the employee sorts himself out. State clearly and unambiguously that, on his return, any discussion of the matter has to be informal, off the premises, and outside working hours.

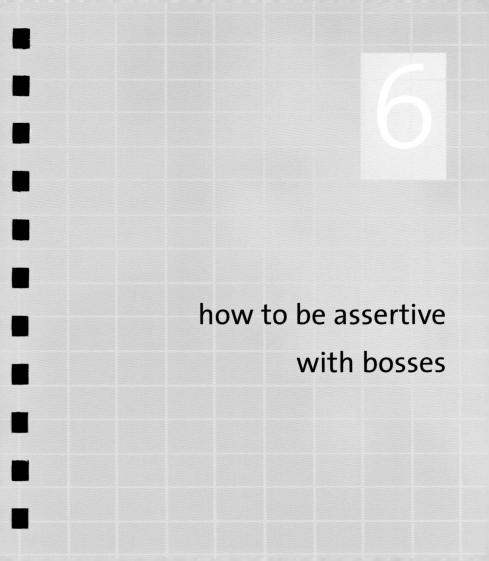

6

how to be assertive
with bosses

how to be assertive with bosses

Refusing requests

Saying "no" to requests from a boss is one of the most difficult things for employees for several reasons:

1 As companies keep reducing staff numbers, there is an unwritten rule that the surviving employees need to take over other tasks. Refusing to do this could lead to firing.

2 The boss will hold it against those who refuse for lack of cooperation and negativity.

3 Those employees feel guilty that by saying "no" other colleagues who can't say "no" will be asked and that will raise friction in the team.

4 They will be passed over for future promotions.

5 They have no right to refuse.

THE POSSIBLE CONSEQUENCES OF ACCEPTING REQUESTS:

1   The employee will be asked again as she's seen as a soft touch.

2   The employee who says "yes" but really wants to say "no" will build up resentment for her passive behavior.

3   The employee will do the job badly due to over-commitments and fail to satisfy the boss. This is a lose-lose situation.

4   If you are a middle manager, you may respond aggressively and pass on the extra work to another worker who can't say "no."

Refusing requests continued

TIPS FOR REFUSING REQUESTS ASSERTIVELY

1 Avoid long, profuse apologies. That puts you in a position of feeling guilty. Stick to a fact like "I would rather pass this time."

2 You can try thanking the boss for considering you.

3 If you are going to provide reasons, keep this brief and succinct: "I don't want to take extra work that is going to affect my present assignment. I hope that you understand." It is not wise to cite personal reasons that could affect how your ability to do the job is perceived.

4 Don't promise future favors to make you feel better about this refusal. You are only setting yourself up for future requests.

5 Don't ask for more time as a delaying tactic because this sends a misleadingly hopeful message.

6 Fogging. This means that you literally put up a fog. You show the person requesting help that you acknowledge their need but are unable to comply: "I can see that you need to get that done but as I said, I am not available right now." Using this method leaves you less open to manipulation.

how to be assertive with bosses

Handling criticism

Few people are good at taking criticism lightly. The ways others perceive and regard performance are so intrinsic to work life that if criticism is not given and taken in an assertive way, it can lead to misunderstandings and resentment. The likelihood is that a supervisor is not necessarily going to be assertive in giving criticism so the onus is on you to react assertively.

1

IT'S YOUR BEHAVIOR, NOT PERSONALITY

Most people learn to assume that criticism is a slight on their personality at an early age where it is more difficult to distinguish between a parent's criticism of a specific action and criticism of the self. You have to stand back and unlearn these personal associations. Even if a boss is criticizing you in an aggressive way, try and focus on the comments about your behavior that are being alluded to. A manager who resorts to comments on personality is unlikely to get very far.

2 ACKNOWLEDGE, DON'T DEFEND
How many times have you responded to criticism with a vehement list of reasons why the person making the criticism is wrong? It's a natural defense mechanism used by most people. However, a hurt, argumentative response tends to associate people with guilt. Don't forget that acknowledging the other person's criticism does not mean at this stage that you are agreeing with all the contents. It is simply putting you in the position of a rational adult as opposed to the angry child who's been caught out.

Handling criticism continued

3 QUESTION
Once you have acknowledged the remarks, by all means
question whether the criticism is valid or not. If the criticism is
not specific, try and piece out the facts from the opinion. If
you are still confused, ask for some examples of your behavior.

4 ACCEPT
If there is justification in the criticism, remember that bosses
have a right to request an improvement in your performance
and you have a right to make mistakes. Both actions are part
of working life. "You are right, the way I acted in that instance
made things difficult." Repeating the criticism back may sound
strange to begin with but the control needed makes you look
assertive, in control, and ready to make amends.

5 LOOK FORWARD

A real demonstration that you are taking full responsibility for your actions is to go one step further. "You are right, I haven't spent long enough on the accounts. I am going to draw up a graph to make things clearer."

6 DISAGREE

If the boss fails to explain adequately what your mistakes are and the criticism continues to be general and appears as an attack, then you can disagree. Spell out your objections calmly and briefly: "I can see why you may have come to that conclusion, but if you look closely at x, you will find that...." You may be tempted to use that to criticize back, but that is making you aggressive, not assertive.

Deflecting sensitive criticism

Sensitive criticism refers to remarks that in themselves may be relatively innocuous but that press some buttons in you that make you overreact disproportionately. This is probably because the criticism touches a deep-rooted fear or insecurity, probably stemming from childhood, that the person criticizing you is unaware of.

STEPS TO HANDLE SENSITIVE CRITICISM ASSERTIVELY:

1

WATCH OUT FOR SIGNALS
Can you feel your stomach churning, your heart palpitating, your jaw clenching? Your boss has managed to touch on a raw nerve without meaning to, and you feel hurt. After the meeting, write down exactly what it is from the past that seems to set you off and try to rationalize it. Think of ways in which you have managed to change since then. Do you automatically respond to the signals when they are no longer relevant? Next time the signals come, can you remind yourself that these earlier concerns and worries are no longer valid?

2 BREATHE DEEPLY
Short, quick breaths, followed by longer, deeper breaths will help you in the process of standing back from the sensitive criticism.

3 SEEK POSITIVE INNER THOUGHTS
Turn to positive thoughts and images of another part of your work. Everyone has strengths and weaknesses. Maybe you are overestimating your weaknesses and underestimating your strengths?

Deflecting sensitive criticism continued

4 ACKNOWLEDGE, ACCEPT

Remember that you gain time and composure by acknowledging the criticism. You may even accept the criticism, but you are not necessarily agreeing with it. Ask for time to consider if necessary.

5 REWARD YOURSELF

The more times you can manage to deflect sensitive criticism, the more apt you will become at not responding passively (like feeling crumpled) or aggressively (like lashing out wildly in defense). Congratulate yourself for having looked assertive even when you were hurting. That might take the sting out of future responses to sensitive criticism.

6 REFLECT
If you continue to feel aggrieved by some types of criticism, consider once more whether the pain you go through is worth the content of the original remarks that fired you up. Have you allowed criticism from childhood to gain too much power?

7 LOOK AT THE BROADER PERSPECTIVE
Very often, criticism comes about as a result of poor work performance. If you feel that the odds are always stacked against you at work, consider whether office systems and protocols need to be changed. Take the initiative and meet with your boss to suggest any necessary changes. If successful, the root cause of the criticism will be removed.

how to be assertive with bosses

Receiving praise

Coping with praise in an assertive manner can be as difficult as accepting criticism, for three reasons:

1 It may appear big-headed to agree with praise.

2 The praise may be exaggerated and therefore open to suspicion.

3 It leaves you exposed to envy from competitive colleagues.

THE ASSERTIVE RESPONSE

1 Your boss may learn to receive praise himself while being nonassertive or aggressive.

2 If you feel the praise is justified, accept it more profusely: "Thanks, I appreciate it."

3 Keep a mental note of the praise to add to your list of positive inner thoughts.

Receiving praise continued

4 Well-timed praise is designed to encourage and make
someone else feel good about himself. Remember that
the next time you notice a particularly good job done by
a colleague or subordinate and return the compliment.
Appreciating and respecting others makes them work better.

HOW AGGRESSIVE PEOPLE REACT

1 They use it to boast about their work in general: "It's the least I could expect of myself."

2 They question the validity of the praise: "It was nothing really. What I accomplished last month was far bigger."

3 They put themselves down: "It wasn't really me, it was thanks to the team."

how to be assertive with bosses

Receiving praise continued

HOW PASSIVE PEOPLE REACT

1 They are embarrassed by the praise and deny they had any involvement: "I have to thank Pete in accounts really for all the work."

2 They put themselves down: "It was a fluke really. I'm usually no good at these things."

3 They act the martyr: "Yeah, well, someone had to do it. Might as well have been me."

HOW THE PRAISER FEELS

1 People handing out the praise can feel rejected. They were trying to sound generous and upbeat and were deflated.

2 They can become inhibited about handing out praise to avoid the experience of rejection.

3 They may learn to receive praise themselves in nonassertive or aggressive ways.

how to be assertive with bosses

Raises and promotions

Assertiveness is essential when asking for a raise or promotion, especially as you have to sell yourself without sounding arrogant or unreasonable.

TIPS TO FOLLOW

1

RIGHTS
It is your right to ask for a salary raise or promotion.
Remember that the boss also has a right to refuse.

2

CHOOSE YOUR TIME
If you've been priming yourself to ask for a raise for some time, wait for a period when you have particularly shone to approach the boss. The timing of the actual interview is also important. Make sure it is an appropriate moment for the boss. Is she able to give the matter her full attention?

3 BE SPECIFIC
Be armed with evidence for the promotion or raise and also
with approximate figures that make sense.

4 BE READY TO COMPROMISE
Being assertive means accepting the limitations of any
situation. If you manage to achieve half your objectives,
accept that as a victory of sorts.

Raises and promotions continued

5 ASK QUESTIONS

If your request for a higher salary is turned down, don't just inwardly groan, nor should you start threatening the boss. Ask what steps you can take to deserve a raise, perhaps by taking on more projects, or taking responsibility for developing your team, or any extra training that your boss feels would be appropriate. It shows you are willing to take positive action and to improve if necessary.

6 LOOK FORWARD

Accept any decision that has been arrived at reasonably, but try to pin your boss down to a review of the situation in the near future (no longer than six months away, for example). This shows the boss that your request was not an ill-considered chance but an indication that you value your work and are prepared to work for your right to improve yourself and your status.